"Send for Haym Salomon!"

HAYM SALOMON
Courtesy of Haym Salomon Home for the Aged, Brooklyn, N.Y.

Gift of Mrs. H. Altshiler

"Send for Haym Salomon!"

BY VICK KNIGHT, JR.

Illustrated by Joseph M. Henninger

HAYM SALOMON FOUNDATION

in collaboration with

BORDEN PUBLISHING COMPANY

Alhambra, California

for B.P. and John Pollack

from Ginny Knight

with regards of the author

First Edition

Vick Knight Jr

December 1976

Table of Contents

IN APPRECIATION

The author gratefully acknowledges the assistance given in the writing and researching of this volume by many individuals and institutions. He is particularly appreciative of the help provided by the staff of the Library of the Irvine campus of the University of California, the Kahn Memorial Library of the Jewish Community Council in Los Angeles, California, the National Archives of the Library of Congress and the American Jewish Historical Society of Waltham, Massachusetts.

Serving as editor has been the author's father, Vick Knight, Sr., a distinguished writer in his own right, who shares with his son a deep respect and admiration for those "Sons of Liberty" who made their dream of a United States of America come true.

General Washington Plans the Attack on Yorktown.

1   *Send for Haym Salomon!*

"Send for Haym Salomon!"
The words came from the mouth of General George Washington.
The spirit sprang from the very soul of a newborn nation struggling to survive its infancy.

"Send for Haym Salomon!"

Already, the junior officers who sat around the makeshift strategy table were beginning to stir, for the words needed no elaboration. Every member of the General Staff was instantly aware of the meaning, the full significance, the importance of Washington's order.

As the officers briskly moved out of the tent to carry out the command, a bystander not aware of the seriousness of the crisis might well have asked "Who *is* this Haym Salomon? And why is it that the grim faces of these military men reflect the indispensable necessity of delivering him to General Washington with the utmost haste?"

But every officer in that room, as resplendent in his pride as he was disheveled in his tattered uniform, knew that the destiny of a nation might very well hang precariously upon a swift and successful consultation with Haym Salomon.

George Washington was faced with finding a minimum of $20,000. Not tomorrow, not next week. Now. Twenty thousand dollars, indeed! Years later, a United States willing to fight to save other independent nations, as it had fought to establish and preserve its own freedom, would engage in wars in which it spent $20,000 *every fifth of a second*, around the clock. But no other single second in the nation's history would produce a result so momentous as this for such a tiny sum of money.

Looking back now, with the perspective of more than 200 years, it could be said with honesty that this may well have been the most important $20,000 in the nation's fiscal history.

Even of temper, and a calm man under the most pressing conditions, Washington had tried to deliver his order without tones or overtones of desperation. Still, he knew, as his men knew. The Continental Army's resources were almost completely exhausted.

The critical year was now, 1781. The War for American Independence—actually an unpopular cause to many of the people—found the Continental Army ragged and hungry, short of arms and ammunition. Even the most dedicated volunteers were beginning to abandon hope.

New York City was occupied by British Redcoats. A number of major harbors had already fallen and others were blockaded by the Royal Navy. Pennsylvania's troops were virtually in a state of mutiny. Many had actually deserted their posts and set out for Philadelphia to demand back pay and food.

Money was so scarce that several members of the Continental Congress faced prison because of their inability to meet their personal debts.

Where, one might ask, were the *Federal* Funds? When a nation is in trouble such as this, doesn't it borrow? Doesn't it resort to deficit financing, mortgaging its future to sustain its present? The truth is, there were no Federal Funds. And the nation had no credit. Each of the 13 Colonies was forced to finance its own soldiers, to feed and arm them as they battled a British Army superior in size, provisions, equipment and fire-power. Washington had depleted every cent he could raise, including a great deal of his own fortune, which was substantial. He had borrowed beyond the limits of his credit. To sustain his army he had, personally signed notes guaranteeing as much as fifty per cent interest.

Washington—this gallant General who now had sent out the call for Haym Salomon—was the leader in the movement for American Independence. He had been named Commander of the Revolutionary Army in 1775, six years before this crisis. It is a matter of record that he accepted the post, but refused payment of a salary for his services. Having himself sacrificed much of what he had, he found it difficult to understand why so many others, including men of vast resources, stood idly by.

General Washington's army, once over 20,000 strong, now had less than 9,000 men. To survive at all required the greatest of military cunning. If the entire army were to be concentrated in one place, it could be wiped out in a single battle. Thus, Washington realized that he must avoid large-scale confrontations with the Redcoats. Many of his engagements were actually strategic retreats, arranged to force the British to chase, to grow weary, to become confused.

Earlier, Washington's officers had told him that the majority of his unpaid soldiers wanted him to solidify the situation by taking over the government and becoming its first king.

American history shines with no brighter example of a man's integrity, unselfishness, and wisdom, than Washington's refusal. All Americans should be proud that their nations's first President was a man who had turned down the invitation to be its first king.

But on this grim day in 1781, Washington's thoughts dwelt not on personal glory of any kind. The key word was "survival," and a minimum of $20,000 stood between him and a military maneuver that could turn the tide. And, he sent for Haym Salomon.

Far into the preceding night, Washington had reviewed the situation privately. Out of his acknowledged genius as a military strategist, combined with scouting reports on enemy troop concentrations, he developed a plan to surprise and trap the southern British forces, under the command of Lord Cornwallis. It was daring. It was filled with great danger. But when Washington unveiled his plan to his staff the following morning, there was immediate agreement. More, there was positive enthusiasm. There were smiles. There was a spirit and an eagerness he was certain would spread to the line troops who must carry out the plan. This was of vital importance, for the troops were as low in morale as they were on supplies.

Secret information supplied by intelligence officers and undercover observers revealed that the southern enemy army was camped in a small tobacco port in Virginia, Yorktown. This mobile British Army appeared to be committed to a general southward movement and was waiting for the British Navy to bring additional men and supplies.

Washington had been able to recruit an excellent field general from France, the Count de Rochambeau. With the combined French and American armies arriving together at Yorktown, it would be possible to surprise the British forces from two sides at once and force them into a pocket between the James River and the seacoast. A victory here could be a decisive thrust in the six long years of war. The French fleet was available to provide a blockade from the sea. It could shift the momentum. The Battle of Yorktown could advance and insure American Independence.

But the Battle of Yorktown might never be fought. The defeat of the British might never come. The one weakness in the brilliant plan was money—twenty thousand dollars.

Immediate activation of the plan was necessary. Given time to organize an offensive drive with the help of the mighty British fleet, the well-equipped and well-fed Redcoats, aided by their hired German troops, could strike at the Americans and possibly turn the tide of the war. Throughout history, armies generously endowed with bravery and brains, have fallen in defeat simply because their governments could not or would not meet the expenses of maintaining and supporting an all-out military effort.

And the Continental Army was not composed of professional

soldiers, but consisted rather of tradesmen, trappers, farmers, parsons, blacksmiths, lawyers and schoolteachers. These were citizen soldiers from almost every walk of life joined in a common cause.

Washington, now 20,000 precious dollars short of the amount needed to carry out his plan to trap Cornwallis, had named Robert Morris his Minister of Finance in 1778. This had proven to be an excellent choice. In the years following the Declaration of Independence, it had become increasingly obvious that success depended greatly upon the Colonies' ability to finance their efforts to gain their freedom.

Were it not for Washington's personal reputation and strong character, the entire revolutionary movement would have earlier collapsed under the mound of unpaid bills. As generals over the years have discovered, Washington eventually learned that it was virtually impossible to devote the required time to military matters while engaging in fund-raising activities. So, he had turned to Robert Morris for help in keeping the financial accounts of the government under practical control.

Morris was considered in those days to be a genius in dealing with money. As one of the Patriots who personally had signed the Declaration of Independence in Philadelphia in 1776, he was known as a tireless fighter for freedom. He demonstrated an ability to obtain funds from a wide variety of sources. And he was able to negotiate loans at most favorable rates of interest. It appeared for a time that his efforts would permit the new nation to meet its obligations and pay its bills. But the situation gradually deteriorated.

As the Minister of Finance, Morris dealt with banks and brokers. He used bills of exchange to meet the government's debts.

Following the Battle of Saratoga in 1778 and the American victory, France had decided to provide funds to help the Colonists against the British. The French had little love for the English. In those days there was no organized system for transferring money through checks drawn on banks. France used "bills of exchange" to enable their American friends to buy supplies and pay their troops. These legal papers bound the French to pay the stated amount of money to anyone who purchased the bills.

Economic conditions in the Colonies were such that it was often difficult to receive full face value for these bills of exchange. Some bankers in America took advantage of this chance to buy the bills at less than face value. They purchased them at a discount and then later obtained the full value through their agents overseas.

This practice cost Robert Morris and the American Patriots huge sums of money that their French allies had originally intended them to have.

Morris enlisted the aid of a young refugee broker in Philadelphia named Haym Salomon to buy and sell bills of exchange for the government at a favorable rate. Salomon's skill in financial matters and reputation for honest dealing proved to be a combination destined to affect the future of the Colonies.

Who was this man? How had he managed to gain the respect and trust of his neighbors and business associates? How had he reached the point where a troubled George Washington would send for him in a last-ditch effort to win a decisive battle and save the United States?

Haym Salomon's early years, and his quest for freedom in his own native land, would provide some clues to the vital services he would later so unselfishly contribute to his adopted country.

2 The Early Years

In the titles and texts of books related to America's beginnings, two words are frequently used to describe the early settlers: seeds and roots. The implication of this figure of speech is that both pilgrim and pioneer came here from distant lands, planted themselves in the rich and fertile American earth and then grew and flourished in a vast garden of liberty and freedom.

One cannot quarrel with this comparison, although it would be less than honest not to admit that some of those seeds would later mature into weeds, rather than beautiful flowers, lush vegetables or mighty oak trees.

For Haym Salomon, a more appropriate word-picture would describe him not as a seed or root, but as a cutting or *scion*, pruned from a growing vine in faraway Poland and sent to America to be grafted to a willing host in the vineyard of Independence.

Indeed, the struggle to achieve freedom was comparable to the native American grape. Its root stock was strong, but as it grew, wild and uncultivated, it produced almost no fruit at all, and that which it did yield was small and bitter rather than sweet. By carefully grafting these New World vines with cuttings from European grapes, large, juicy sweet fruit was produced.

In a similar way, by grafting Haym Salomon to the American Dream, a liberty that languished in the fields began to show new life. Suppose we take a close look at the stock from which this cutting came.

Leszno, later known as Lissa, is located in the western part of Poland in the Province of Poznan, approximately 180 miles West of Warsaw. In 1740, it had close to 3500 residents, among them Haym Salomon's parents.

No records exist today to provide us with an insight into this family whose son born that year would have such a powerful impact upon American history. We do know that the Salomons had settled in Poland after leaving their home in Portugal. People of the Jewish faith in both Spain and Portugal had emigrated in large numbers in that period due to persecution from local authorities which made living conditions impossible for those who loved freedom.

Those who did not leave of their own accord were often driven out by religious fanatics who would not tolerate any faith other than their own. Jews fled to the East in the only direction open to them, and many found refuge in Syria, Palestine and Turkey. Others, including the Salomons, traveled to the northeast and settled in the lands in and around Poland. In many instances, they were forced to live in segregated areas known as ghettos, usually located in the least desirable sections of the community.

In other cases, they transplanted themselves to the culturally backward villages of Eastern Europe where they brought the welcome arts of trade and money-lending to their new homelands.

The Salomons belonged to the Sephardic branch of those descended from the ancient Hebrews, and the family was known to be actively involved in their local Jewish community. Young Haym must have been an attentive student in school; the lessons he learned in Leszno were to influence his life in ways then incapable of being imagined.

With his family, he celebrated and observed the festivals and Holy Days of his heritage: Purim, Passover, Rosh Hashanah, Yom Kippur, Succoth and Hanukkah. He studied and learned to practice the ancient laws of Moses, and became known as one who could be trusted in his relations with others.

A gift for the use of words was early recognized in young Haym, and he was later to master at least six languages. Perhaps the travels of his family to seek a receptive place to set down their roots provided him with an atmosphere where a knowledge of foreign tongues was valued. In any event, we know that this skill was to play an important role in the manner that he was able to adapt to situations and circumstances which he later encountered.

More important to his future activities, however, was his overwhelming desire to live in a free society. This was to take him many thousands of miles from the place of his birth and to affect the lives of millions of men and women, boys and girls, as yet unborn.

Haym Salomon left his home in Poland when he was about twenty years old. He was to spend the next decade traveling about Europe, learning the principles of the business of banking. He seemed to have a natural ability to apply sound financial practices to commercial ventures, and became skilled in exchanging services and goods. It must have amazed much older business associates to learn that a man so young could conduct himself in the marketplace in such a masterful manner. He built for himself a reputation as an expert in dealing with money and one who was always fair and honorable in his tradings with others.

But Haym Salomon missed his family and friends in Poland. He knew that his native land was undergoing a difficult and trying time in its history. Poland had a powerless and indecisive king, and the country was in serious and immediate danger of being divided into fragments by the stronger neighboring armies of Russia, Austria and Prussia. King Frederick II of Prussia had proposed a division to Catherine the Great of Russia and Maria Theresa of Austria. In 1768, while the young Salomon was still learning his trade, the Confederation of Bar was organized to attempt to liberate Poland from foreign control and influence.

Casimir Pulaski, at 21, became a national hero as he commanded Polish soldiers to victory in several battles against Russian troops. The son of wealthy and aristocratic parents, Pulaski became the leader of a group of patriots who dedicated their lives and fortunes to freeing the land of their birth from the occupying armies.

A plan was developed in 1771 to abduct King Stanislas. Pulaski led a small party of conspirators whose intention was to capture the ruler in his palace and carry him off to a secret place. He would be kept there until he either agreed to launch a firm defense of his country or withdraw as king. The conspiracy began successfully, and the monarch was being taken to a prearranged hiding place, when an unexpected event occurred.

Soldiers loyal to the weak king suddenly appeared on the scene, and Pulaski and his men were forced to flee.

The patriots were in disgrace. Pulaski and his fellow plotters had failed in their bold effort to liberate their homeland. They were lucky to escape with their lives.

Haym Salomon's name cannot be definitely identified today by historians who try to link him with Pulaski's vain attempt to save Poland. What is known for certain is that he left there under circumstances which strongly suggest that he was indeed deeply involved in the futile but noble effort. The timing of his departure and his later demonstrations of both bravery and patriotism make him a prime candidate for involvement in the unsuccessful abduction attempt.

He was a stateless individual now, forced along with many others to leave Poland. Some of these men without a country settled in France, where Pulaski was later briefly imprisoned for his failure to pay his debts. Thaddeus Kosciuszko, another exiled Pole, was studying engineering in Paris at the time. He had been sent to France by wealthy Polish friends who provided him with funds to attend school. Internal affairs had also made it impossible for him now to return home. Salomon, Pulaski and Kosciuszko were all ultimately to cross the vast Atlantic and take part in

16

America's fight for independence. They most likely saw in this struggle an obvious parallel to their own country's attempt to gain her liberty.

Salomon had the option of settling in any of several lands open to Jewish immigrants at the time. His ability to speak various languages coupled with his skill in financial matters would provide him with the tools necessary to become successful almost anywhere he chose to live.

The British Colonies in America beckoned to him. He wanted to end his wanderings and plant his roots in a permanent and receptive location. He undoubtedly thought of marrying and having a family of his own.

From all that he had heard, this America must truly be the land of opportunity and prosperity that he had hoped to find.

Haym Salomon stayed in England only long enough to assemble the funds he needed to book passage to New York City and sailed in August of 1772. Along with other immigrants, he found himself crossing the Atlantic Ocean while crowded on a ship smaller than the ferry boats that now serve tourists visiting the Statue of Liberty.

He was never again to set his eyes on his beloved homeland, but his longing for freedom was to stay with him all the remaining days of his life.

Haym Salomon's First View of New York's Busy Harbor.

3 To New York City

When Haym Salomon first set foot on the soil of the New World, he was 32 years old and had already exhibited an ability to be both resourceful and adaptable to changing circumstances. He must have known that this colonial land would provide him with abundant opportunities to use the skills and knowledge that he had acquired in his earlier travels.

He must have sensed that the climate was such that he would be able to grow and prosper. And New York City provided just the conditions necessary for such a flourishing.

The most populated part of New York City was located at the southern tip of Manhattan Island, below what is still known today as Wall Street. At the time that Salomon lived and worked there, a portion of the deteriorated wall that had provided the street its name still survived in place. Dutch styled houses reminded the visitor of the fact that the fortified colony once known as New Amsterdam had been originally established here in

19

1625 after representatives of the Dutch West India Company had purchased the land from the Indians. Little did anyone then suspect that this settlement reportedly bought for $24 worth of trinkets would eventually become a great nation's largest city and chief seaport.

In 1772 it was a thriving community of some 14,000 residents. New York had been renamed in honor of the Duke of York and now paid allegiance to the Union Jack as the capital of the British Colony bearing its name.

Historians today tend to believe that Salomon was the first Jew of Polish birth to emigrate to America. If this is true, he joined a concentration of approximately 3000 other Jewish Colonists who had preceded him to the New World in the pursuit of happiness. Theirs was not a ghetto existence, as often was the case in the Europe they had left behind, for they were now free citizens engaged in commercial, professional and related fields. In contrast to ghetto restrictions, they were free to come and go at will.

King George III of Great Britain considered the Colonies to exist only to provide food, supplies and money for his widespread kingdom. Almost everything shipped to the American ports was heavily taxed. This was bitterly resented by His Majesty's otherwise loyal subjects. Taxes without any opportunity for representation was a difficult pill for them to swallow. The Colonists contended that governments should gain their just powers from the consent of the governed.

Following the end of the nine-year French and Indian War in early 1763, Great Britain vastly increased its land holdings in North America. France gave up all future claims to Canada as well as to those portions of Louisiana lying East of the mighty Mississippi River. The long and bloody war proved also to be a costly one for the British as it added close to $500 million to that nation's already staggering debts. New ways of raising funds had to be developed, and the King's advisors suggested that added revenue could be raised easily by levying new and heavier taxes on certain materials sold to the Colonies.

In 1765, the British Parliament passed what was to become known as the Stamp Act. This measure was designed to raise

20

about $300,000 a year to be used to help reduce England's national indebtedness. The Stamp Act required the Colonists' payment for special revenue stamps on such commonly used items as legal documents, newspapers, playing cards, pamphlets and almanacs.

As often happens when people are unhappy with the conditions under which they are forced to live, a group was formed to try to improve citizens' rights. These men selected a name which proved to be descriptive of the role they were to play in their homeland's future. They called themselves the "Sons of Liberty." Patrick Henry, Alexander Hamilton and Samuel Adams were among their leaders.

Their main goal was to obtain fair treatment for themselves and their fellow Colonists. Many considered them to be Patriots working in the best interest of all concerned; others frankly thought of them as troublemakers who should be jailed immediately as dangerous radicals. The majority of wealthier citizens were "Loyalists" and remained true to the King, even though they often quietly agreed among themselves that taxes were getting out of hand and a greater voice in their own affairs would be appreciated. After all, the English Constitution guaranteed that "no man can justly take the Property of another without his Consent." The Stamp Act was never a very popular piece of legislation and, even following its eventual repeal, continued to cause bad feelings among the Colonists.

Nine of the Thirteen Colonies sent delegates to New York City in October 1765 to protest the Stamp Act. Gathering not far from where Haym Salomon would later establish his place of business, they underscored their displeasure by voting to oppose the importation of any of the goods affected by the new taxes. Their objection was to the specific taxes, and also to the circumstances of taxation without representation.

"Sons of Liberty" groups had been originally established in Boston, Philadelphia, New York and other cities primarily to oppose and resist the newly-imposed British levies. The Stamp Act Congress held in the Fall of 1765 probably had members of one or more of the "Sons of Liberty" chapters serving as delegates.

In the Spring of the following year, the British Parliament reacted to pressures from the Colonies and took action to replace the Stamp Act with another equally unpopular tax. This new revenue was designed to collect a surcharge on tea, glass, paper, lead, oil and paint. It was known as the Townshend Act and named for Charles Townshend, the English Chancellor of the Exchequer. This Act was expected to raise $200,000 in taxes from American consumers.

The New York "Sons of Liberty" led the local protests against these new British taxes. Their membership came from all walks of life, although the nature of their activities made most of them unwilling to be publicly identified with their affiliation. We know now that their rolls included Isaac Sears, John Lamb, Gersham Mott, Jacobus van Zandt and Alexander MacDougall.

MacDougall was later to become a close associate of Haym Salomon, and is believed to be the man who originally recruited him into joining the "Sons of Liberty."

On March 5, 1770, while Salomon was still in Europe, a confrontation took place on the Boston waterfront between British soldiers and local citizens. Snow and ice covered the streets, and the bad weather was matched by the bad mood of those assembled. The Colonists were fired upon by the Redcoats, and five civilians later died as a result of gunshot wounds. This incident soon became known as the "Boston Massacre," and was used by Patriots as evidence of the cruel manner in which the British were treating the Colonists. Samuel Adams pointed to the deaths of these five Americans to illustrate his conclusion that his countrymen must immediately arm themselves in defense against the occupying Redcoats. He was joined by men such as Paul Revere in writing and distributing leaflets advocating boycott of all taxed goods and attacking the existing English rule. Today, in the very shadows of the Old State House, the fateful events of this day are marked by a circle of cobblestones. Echoes of these shots rang all the way up and down this string of Colonies clinging to a coastline.

The unpopular Townshend Act was soon repealed, but the British Parliament continued to impose its tax on tea.

4 The Sons of Liberty

In late 1773, almost two years after Haym Salomon arrived in New York, a group of Massachusetts citizens dressed themselves as Indians and assembled at Boston's crowded harbor. In protest of the Tea Act, they boarded the British ships "Dartmouth," "Eleanor" and "Beaver," moored at Griffin's Wharf, and tossed 342 chests of tea into the chilled waters of Boston Bay. Boston Harbor turned into a teapot that night. This quickly became known as the "Boston Tea Party" and served to add fuel to the existing fires of protest in the Thirteen Colonies.

By this time, Salomon had already opened offices on New York City's Broad Street and was building his reputation as a broker.

He had arrived in America with little if any funds of his own, so he must have convinced others to lend him the money to establish himself as a commission merchant. There is no doubt that he prospered in his new venture. He soon became known as one extremely well qualified to conduct a financial business.

He is described in letters of that time as a small man with a soft-spoken voice and a gentle bearing. His manners and his speech reflected his European background. He undoubtedly had many opportunities to use his acquired skills in French, Italian, Russian, German and Polish in his business dealings with the English-speaking Colonists and others who utilized his brokerage services. He found himself called upon to act as an interpreter to translate for other immigrants who wished to conduct business but had not as yet learned to speak English.

It did not take Salomon very long to observe that there were many similarities between his new home and the land of his birth. In place of a weak Polish king, the Colonies were ruled by an unstable and wavering British Parliament, unable to decide on matters of grave importance to those they governed, unwilling to listen to sound advice on reasonable solutions for their problems. The very rights that Colonists had come to the New World to enjoy were being denied them by a government an ocean away. Haym Salomon and others had not left their troubled homelands across the sea with intentions to live under like conditions. They sought freedom here. They were willing to do whatever was necessary to maintain their independence and achieve self-government.

Delegates from all of the Thirteen Colonies except Georgia met in Philadelphia in September of 1774 for the first session of the Continental Congress.

Before the second Congress could be called to order, the first battle of what was to be the Revolutionary War was fought.

It really wasn't a battle at all, but rather a minor skirmish of no great military significance. Massachusetts was the scene of this action which took place on the village green at Lexington. A column of 700 Redcoats was on its way to Concord where its mission was to capture and destroy rebel arms and ammunition thought to be stored there. On the morning of April 19, 1775, they were confronted by a band of less than 70 Colonists.

Groups of New England residents had been preparing for a

possible British attack. They had trained themselves to be ready to defend their homes on a minute's notice. For this reason, they were known as "Minutemen."

The night prior to the confrontation, three horsemen had left Boston and ridden through the countryside to alert their neighbors in villages along the way that the Redcoats were about to attack. These three riders were William Dawes, a tanner, Dr. Samuel Prescott, and a well-known silversmith and engraver named Paul Revere. It is a matter of record that Revere owned no horse. He borrowed one from a Deacon named Larkin.

Who fired the first shots at Lexington has never been determined, but 18 Minutemen were either killed or wounded. It was not long before both the British and the Americans knew that they were about to be engaged in a war that would be both lengthy and bloody.

Joining the "Sons of Liberty" was an obvious act for Salomon. His experience in Poland and his desire to live the life of a free man in America left him no other choice.

The decision proved to be a costly one, not only in terms of the effect such an action might have on his growing business, but also in light of how it would change his life and personal freedom.

Haym Salomon's wealthier clients were probably unsympathetic with the motives of the "Sons of Liberty." They were among the privileged class of citizens who suffered the least under the British rule. They supported the monarch (though they sometimes privately referred to him as "German George") and considered all outspoken opponents to be disloyal traitors to the Crown.

At a New York waterfront site known as the Battery, 21 cannon were in position with their barrels pointed toward the sea channel. It was exactly the correct number for a royal salute.

On June 25, 1776, a delegation from the "Sons of Liberty" crossed the Hudson River to welcome General George Washington. The General appointed Philip John Schuyler as commander of New York City's Colonial troops. One of Schuyler's first acts was to remove the Battery's cannon and reposition them where they could be used to defend the region

North of the city. A British man-of-war, the gunship *Asia*, was anchored in the North River a short distance away. Its crew watched in amazement as the "Sons of Liberty" labored in the hot sun to strip the Battery of all 21 guns.

Young Alexander Hamilton and John Lamb were apparent ringleaders among those dismantling the cannon and it is probable that Haym Salomon played a part in the exercise.

By the time *Asia* could turn her guns on the Battery, load and fire, the "Sons" had fled with no losses. It was a triumph for the Patriots, but the identity of the rebels was no longer a secret.

A pamphlet written earlier that year by Thomas Paine and titled *Common Sense* was having a powerful effect upon many Americans who read it. Paine argued that it was only plain common sense that England was no more suited to govern the Colonies than a satellite was fit to control the sun. He said that the American continent should cut itself free from the much smaller British islands. A committee which included John Adams, Benjamin Franklin and Thomas Jefferson was assigned the task of writing a Declaration of Independence from Great Britain. Jefferson assumed the role of principal author of this document which stressed the rights of humans over the rights of property.

On July 2, 1776, a resolution was passed by the Congress meeting in Philadelphia dissolving all connections between the Colonists and the English. Two days later, on July the Fourth, the United Colonies officially became the United States upon adoption of the Declaration of Independence.

In the meantime, the British General, Sir William Howe, had been forced by the Colonists to retreat from Boston. He then concentrated English hopes and manpower upon New York where he expected to find a more sympathetic population. Washington made several attempts to meet and defeat the Redcoats, but his untrained and undermanned citizen soldiers were badly mauled on August 27, 1776, at the Battle of Long Island. He was forced to leave New York City to be entered and occupied by the British.

Both Washington and his second-in-command, General Nathanael Greene, seriously considered burning New York City and leaving the British only ashes following their evacuation. There was ample reason to act in this manner; had not soldiers of the Crown burned Charlestown in order to keep it from falling intact into Patriot hands? What about the destruction that took place at Falmouth and Norfolk? Burning New York would only give the British a fiery taste of their own medicine! Putting the torch to a city was not an unusual act of war in those days nor has this practice been completely eliminated in other wars fought in more recent times.

On September 15, 1776, Sir William Howe led his troops into New York City and took possession for King George III and England. Five days later, the city was in flames.

The fire was ignited in the middle of the night and raced unchecked through one-fourth of the city. Wooden houses and shops went up in flames. Perhaps as many as 400 structures were destroyed by the time dawn broke over the Island of Manhattan.

While the identity of those responsible for the blaze was never positively proven, the British were certain the "Sons of Liberty" were to blame.

Suspected members of the rebel group were hunted down and shot only because they happened to have a flint and steel in their pockets. Possession of anything capable of serving as a match was all the proof the British needed. Others who previously had openly expressed support of the "Sons of Liberty," or were known to have friends among the group's membership, were immediately arrested and thrown into prison. The very freedom they had coveted was now denied them.

Haym Salomon was one such person taken in chains from his home and jailed. The exact reason for his arrest has been lost in the two centuries since, but it was certainly a result of his open friendship with members of the group. It was a time when such associations were considered ample proof of the ability to commit almost any crime, including the attempt to burn down an entire town.

Whatever the reason, Salomon found himself locked up behind prison bars before the final embers of the fire had cooled.

British Troops Arrest a "Son of Liberty."

5 The Provost

The precise charge against Salomon as he was arrested and imprisoned by British troops is lost in history. It may be logically presumed that his candid association and obvious alignment with the "Sons of Liberty" had made him a prime candidate for detention and confinement. This much we know for certain: following seizure, Salomon and his fellow-patriots, taken into custody in the wake of the burning of New York City, were summarily carted off to "gaol," as British history records it. "Gaol" is a British spelling of "jail," and pronounced the same.

This particular lock-up was known as "Old Sugar House." It was indeed a very old building, confiscated by the Redcoats and hastily converted into a makeshift jail for enemies of the Crown.

Originally a warehouse, this dilapidated structure had fallen into almost complete disrepair. Its ancient roof leaked like a tea strainer, and the chill Autumn rains filtered through unchecked on the prisoners. For days and nights on end, Salomon and his fellow inmates sat or lay soaked to their very bones by rain and sleet. Many had fevers. Not even token minimal medical attention was provided. Some died.

Salomon soon developed a stubborn chest cold, with a hacking and painful cough that he was unable to control. Those arrested with him following the fiery destruction of New York City shared his misery, his discomfort. And over the hopes of all of them hovered a fear for their lives, and a fear for the destiny of the land and the liberty they cherished.

In the grim cells of the makeshift jail—totally unlighted except for occasional slivers of light coming through holes in the roof—days and nights were essentially the same, the murkiness broken only when guards appeared now and again to bring the crusts of stale bread and water that posed as meals.

But very early one morning, even before the sun had crept up in the East behind Old Sugar House, two armed guards opened the door and called out the name of Haym Salomon. He arose stiffly from where he lay on the damp, bare wooden floor. Though his voice was hardly audible, so weak had his body become, he responded vocally.

No other prisoner uttered a sound. And yet, the identical sinister thought must have raced through every brain, for every man there knew that Salomon was about to be taken to a place even more dreaded than that which they now endured.

Haym Salomon was on his way to The Provost.

Unlike Old Sugar House, The Provost was not just an ordinary building taken over and converted into a jail for the Redcoats' foes. This was a maximum security prison, designed to hold those condemned to death. And if its own name was a symbol to make any Patriot fearful, the fame of its Warden carried again as much impact. For William Cunningham's name was virtually a synonym for brutality.

By British Army edict, William Cunningham exercised absolute authority at The Provost. He was a tyrant of the first order, a sadistic persecutor who, upon the slightest provocation, would commission acts of extreme torture on his prisoners. His reputation for cruelty extended far beyond the prison walls. And Haym Salomon knew, as he entered the gates of this living Hell, that he was now faced with the supreme crisis of his young life.

Warden Cunningham's immoral treatment of his prisoners was

compounded by his enormous greed. For example, while his captives tried to remain alive on sub-starvation rations, Cunningham slyly diverted the intended food to storage quarters outside the prison. Later, entirely for personal gain, he would sell the food supplies, leaving those jailed meager helpings of watery soup and moldy bread. Only the strongest survived. It is said that Cunningham's actions brought about death by starvation for more than two thousand prisoners under his command at The Provost.

Borderline starvation was only one of Salomon's challenges. He and the other captured Patriots had to contend with many conditions which were barely tolerable: The Provost's dungeons had been built without windows or other ventilation. While this alone would not necessarily prove a serious threat to life, sanitary conditions compounded the problem. Only a single toilet served a large number of men, and the cells were continually damp. More and more prisoners were crowded into the available space as the Redcoats arrested others thought to be plotting against the Crown. At night, there was actually inadequate room for all to lie down to sleep. So a system of rotation and sleeping in shifts had to be arranged by inmates sharing the dungeon. Salomon's cough grew worse. He began to suffer from deep and recurring chest pains. If he were to survive and escape the twin threats of either dying from starvation or being hanged, then he must act quickly.

Crises cause some individuals to lose control of themselves and falter. With others, the zero hour will often serve to bring out their best.

The written language of the Chinese utilizes two drawings which are combined to represent the character meaning "crisis." When used alone, they depict "danger" and "opportunity." While the merchant broker from Poland probably did not know of this, he certainly comprehended the concept involved. He was now able to seize upon a dangerous opportunity. This was to bring about a turning point in his life.

Haym Salomon was to observe, in time, that the German soldiers were for the most part prisoners of the English themselves. They had been drafted against their will by their own Hessian rulers and rented to serve as British soldiers. They had no desire to fight in a war thousands of miles from their homes and families. They were paid little and were often dejected over the circumstances which had brought them to the New World.

Salomon, the Polish Jew, was quick to identify with their sadness. He sensed in this a rare opportunity to strike a blow for liberty—his own as well as that of the hired German troops.

Having no understanding of the German language, the British officers had great difficulty in communicating with their German-born mercenary troops. But German was one of several tongues mastered by Salomon while learning his trade in Europe. Cunningly, he did not offer his services to his jailers as an interpreter. Rather, he meekly demonstrated his skill. The bait was snapped up. Salomon soon found himself busily occupied in his new capacity as the answer to the British language problems with their German troops. This was to prove to be a real triumph.

Now that he could be of some special use to his captors, Salomon was fed much better. He was assigned to one of The Provost's more comfortable cells. He was not yet able to rid himself of his persistent cough, but his health otherwise was gradually restored under improved living conditions. And though he was still very much a prisoner, Salomon could now breathe fresh air. And he generally avoided the sadistic treatment of William Cunningham and his men.

Salomon knew that Pennsylvania, in a bold move to neutralize enemy strength, had made a generous offer to the Germans. The State volunteered to give up to 100 acres of farm land free and clear to any mercenary soldier who would desert the British and promise not to take up arms against the Colonists again. Salomon safely reasoned that this was powerful bait to dangle before men who were natives of a country in which the hope of owning private land was at best a dream. He knew this enticing offer would be a difficult one to refuse.

Starting cautiously, choosing only those Germans he felt confident were the most likely to be receptive to such an opportunity, Salomon began to carry out his dangerous plan.

Salomon quickly discerned that those who were younger and had not as yet started families were immediately attracted to this chance to gain their freedom. True, there were definite risks. If caught, deserters were certain to face a British firing squad. The Germans also considered the possibility that Salomon was not telling the truth. Perhaps it was only a clever plot to trick them into the Continental Army, where their lives quite possibly would be in even greater danger than they presently were.

The Pole must have been a persuasive salesman for Pennsylvania land. It is believed that he was personally responsible for several hundred desertions in just a few months' time. This mass defection was of great concern to the British, but fortunately they did not know that it was caused by Salomon, working behind the scenes to foment the problems with their hired German soldiers. Had the British been aware of the role he played in the defection of these troops, it is probable that both Salomon and the deserting mercenaries would have died at the hands of the hangman.

But surviving by his wits was a technique Salomon had necessarily perfected throughout his life. He continued to be successful in outwitting his British captors.

Indeed, Salomon's performance as official interpreter so impressed the British officers that he was eventually released from The Provost on parole.

Relatively free now, he immediately began to pick up the pieces of his life. He sought to reestablish himself in the mainstream of New York's business community.

Salomon's comeback was challenged by unanticipated obstacles. Old friends crossed the street when they saw him approaching. Because he had been paroled, some merchants considered him a favored friend of the Crown. This he had to suffer in silence, for if he were to let his scuttling of the German mercenaries become public knowledge, it would mean going back to prison, probably to the gallows or the firing squad. Fortunately, the busy port of New York provided him with an excellent base of operations for his new business ventures. He made new friends. And, as in the past, Haym Salomon proved to be the equal to the task at hand.

Salomon Learns That Gold is a Universal Language.

6 Rachel Franks

Salomon's parole placed him in the service and under the jurisdiction of a Hessian General named Heister, and his usefulness as an interpreter apparently led to having most of his restraints lifted by the English. He moved his offices from 222 Broad Street, near the Post Office, across the street to a larger location at 245, closer to City Hall and the center of commerce.

On January 2, 1777, shortly after his release from The Provost, he married Rachel Franks. She was the daughter of Moses Benjamin Franks, a successful and respected merchant with extensive dealings in both New York City and Philadelphia. Her brother, Isaac Franks, though only 19, was a Lt. Colonel on General Washington's staff. Her father had previously been honored for services rendered to both the German Crown of Hanover and that of Great Britain. Her Uncle Jacob and his son, David, had been appointed agents for the British Colonies to the North. She was 15 years of age at the time of their marriage, and Salomon was 36.

The Polish immigrant's career in business now took him in a

new direction, perhaps as a result of aid from Rachel's family. He began to specialize in providing services as a "sutler," or one who furnishes goods and provisions to the armed forces and others in similar need. He was called upon to sell to the occupying British troops, and this may well have resulted in circumstances which would then permit him to serve as a spy for the Americans.

In 1778, he placed an announcement in both the *New York Gazette* and the *Weekly Advertiser* describing himself as a merchant who was capable of providing food and equipment for sailing vessels docked at that busy port. The advertisement stated confidently that "Captains of ships and others can depend upon being supplied on most reasonable terms."

Salomon soon began to prosper and to expand his business of buying and selling merchandise. His familiarity with the currency of foreign lands developed during his years of travel in Europe, and his quickly acquired knowledge of current rates of exchange no doubt served him well. It is certain that his ability to speak several European languages provided him with ample opportunities to converse with a wide range of international seafarers. This gave him an insight into economic trends and commercial information of a similarly valuable nature.

Through it all, he carried on his work with the "Sons of Liberty." He continued in his efforts to convince Hessian soldiers to desert their posts as hired British fighters and become Colonists themselves. It is believed that his growing contacts made it possible for him and his friends to smuggle both men and military intelligence across British lines to Washington's nearby outposts. These were dangerous deeds on his part, as they would be considered acts of treason should they be disclosed, and the penalty for such was death.

His fear of the consequences must have been less than his love for liberty as he maintained his manipulation of the British.

The Hessian General Heister could not have suspected what was going on under his very nose. Likely he and the Redcoats were too involved in their own plots and schemes to consider this small, mannerly, brown-eyed Jew much of a threat to His Majesty's Army.

36

Outside of the Thirteen Colonies, much of the rest of what we know today as the United States of America was unconcerned over this hard-fought struggle for human rights.

Great portions of land were either Indian Reserves or in Spanish hands, and thousands of square miles were as yet unexplored or unoccupied by pioneers. Father Junipero Serra did not found the first of his California missions until 1769 when he erected a crude brushwood shelter near the beautiful harbor of San Diego. Captain John Cook was not to discover what he named the "Sandwich Islands," and we call Hawaii, until 1778. When George Vancouver charted the southeast coast of Alaska in 1791, he found that Russian settlers had already established their territorial claims. In the Spring of 1769, Daniel Boone and his younger brother, Squire, helped to blaze the Wilderness Trail and open a new area known then as Transylvania and now as Kentucky.

But to those under the gun, to those whose lives were daily threatened by the occupying forces of King George III, the War for Independence was a clear and present danger to their safety. British soldiers were quartered in their homes against their will, they were denied the traditional right of free speech, and many of their personal liberties were curtailed. They were subject to searches of their persons and property in the middle of the night, and unreasonable punishment often followed what was really no trial at all.

Haym Salomon knew this. And yet, he continued in his hazardous activities.

The cough he had first noticed while imprisoned in the damp confines of the Old Sugar House and The Provost grew no better and began to worry his young wife. Neither of them realized at the time that he had developed what was then called consumption, an infection of the lungs we know today as tuberculosis.

Still other members of the "Sons of Liberty" were active behind American lines. In Boston, these included Samuel Adams and James Otis; in Delaware, Caesar Rodney; in Virginia, Patrick Henry and Richard Henry Lee; in South Carolina, Thomas Lynch and Christopher Gadsden; and in unoccupied New York,

Salomon's friends, Isaac Sears and Alexander MacDougall.

The resourceful Polish Jew soon found an ally in a French prisoner named Samuel Demezes, and the two of them assisted both French and Americans to escape their British captors.

Things, meanwhile, were not going too well for the Redcoats. On Christmas night in 1776, Washington and his troops boldly crossed the Delaware River into New Jersey, surprising and capturing the British garrison at Trenton. A few days later, the Americans soundly defeated another English force at Princeton. General Howe then decided that firm action must be taken to put down these upstart Colonists. He sailed with a portion of his well-fed and well-dressed British regiments in their powdered wigs and splendid uniforms on his way to occupy the American capital at Philadelphia. The Patriots failed in their gallant attempts to protect the City of Brotherly Love, and British victories at Brandywine and Germantown assured the loss of government headquarters for the budding nation.

Washington was unsuccessful in his subsequent efforts to drive Howe and his men from Philadelphia. Members of the Continental Congress were forced to resume their interrupted sessions in York, Pennsylvania. That Winter, the American General was obliged to camp at Valley Forge, about twenty miles from the abandoned capital. It was a freezing Winter, and Washington's 4000 troops starved and suffered while Howe's 20,000 Redcoats comfortably established themselves in a not-too-unfriendly Philadelphia. The city at the time was the largest English-speaking community outside of London, with 30,000 of the Colonies' total estimated population of less than three million. Howe's troops swelled the size of Philadelphia and discovered to their delight that many of the residents of the Quaker City were Tories, sympathetic to the Loyalist cause. It proved to be an altogether peaceful Winter for the British, but this was the calm before the storm. On the Spring horizon was the unexpected start of a series of misfortunes that plagued the Redcoats the remainder of the war. Had they selected to leave the comforts of their snug quarters in the occupied American capital in January or February, it is probable that they could have handily destroyed the ragged

Patriot troops struggling to survive the bitter Winter at Valley Forge.

Howe unwisely decided to wait until Spring, counting on the Winter elements to take their toll of the brave but starving Colonists. He did not know at the time, but he was later destined to face not only Washington but a clever adversary in the form of a newly recruited Prussian officer named Baron Frederich William von Steuben.

While the British forces spent the first few months of 1778 holding festive dances and parties in cozy Philadelphia, Steuben quietly undertook his duties as Instructor General of the Continental Forces. The men he trained in the ways of war were anything but professional soldiers, yet this Prussian, expert in war strategy and lover of liberty, taught them the military skills necessary to meet the Redcoats on their own terms. In the awful cold and misery of Valley Forge, he drilled them to use muskets, bayonets and cannon to best advantage. When Spring came and their ranks were swelled with dedicated recruits from nearby farming communities, Steuben and Washington no longer commanded green troops. The men had survived terrible hardships. They had trained diligently. They were now ready and willing to take on the best the Crown had to offer.

On June 18, the Redcoats, now under the command of Sir Henry Clinton, departed from their Winter sanctuary in Philadelphia and marched towards a reunion with those they had left behind in New York City.

That very same day, Haym Salomon placed a small advertisement in the New York Gazette offering for sale a variety of provisions including "white wine and vinegar."

Ten days later, General Washington and his augmented forces under General Charles Lee attacked the British at Monmouth Court House in New Jersey. The hardened veterans of Valley Forge and their newly expanded ranks met the English troops on a burning hot day.

The American assault was courageous but unsuccessful. One of the most moving individual acts in the young nation's history took place on this battlefield and involved a determined Colonist named Mary Ludwig Hays. While carrying water to the thirsty men at arms, she learned that her husband had fallen in action. She is credited with manning his cannon throughout the balance of the battle. Her gallant and daring exploit gave her the nickname of "Molly Pitcher" and served to symbolize the important and often unheralded role played by numerous brave women in the struggle for independence.

After costly losses to both sides, Clinton withdrew and headed for Sandy Hook, where his men boarded ships and returned to New York. The Patriots did not win the battle; it was more of a draw. But the British had abandoned Philadelphia and now recognized the fact that the Colonists had indeed developed a formidable fighting force. Coupled with a stunning defeat the previous Autumn at Saratoga in upperstate New York, where General "Gentleman Johnny" Burgoyne had lost or surrendered 7000 men to the Americans, the British had now come to the realization that the tide of war had turned.

The French had by this time entered the conflict, although this alliance was yet to have the desired results on the outcome of hostilities.

7 *Condemned to Death*

In early July, Rachel Franks Salomon gave birth to her first child, a boy named Ezekiel. The Salomons had only a few weeks together to enjoy their son as pressures were again mounting to imprison the slender Jewish businessman. Rumors led the British to take it for granted that Washington was preparing to follow Clinton and attack New York City.

It is probable that earlier suspicions of Salomon's true leanings and presumed service as a secret agent of the Americans caused the Redcoats to arrest him once again. They may have assumed that he was part of an imagined plot to set the torch to the city, or he may have become careless in his efforts to assist escaped prisoners in joining the Patriots' rosters.

In any event, the first week of August found British soldiers in their high pointed hats escorting Haym Salomon back to The Provost. They were preceded by a drummer beating a slow cadence so that all who heard and observed the procession could comprehend the full power of the Crown.

He was taken to the dreaded Provost. This time, Warden William Cunningham assigned him to a section known as "Congress

Hall" since it had housed so many distinguished Patriot prisoners. Those confined here rarely returned to their families and friends. Detainment in Congress Hall was often a mere formality prior to a prejudged verdict of "guilty" and the gallows.

Less than a week later, Salomon was taken before a military court martial. It was presided over by Sir Henry Clinton, no doubt still smarting over the failure of the British to defeat the Americans at Monmouth where his troops were forced to flee to the safety of New York City. The trial was held in a brick building facing the present location of the Statue of Liberty, but liberty was hardly on the minds of those sitting in Salomon's judgment. There was no jury present, and the accused did not have the services of a defense counsel. In times of war, normal laws do not always apply. Haym Salomon was charged with being a spy, with sheltering other spies and escaped prisoners, with promoting the desertion of Hessian soldiers and with a long list of treasonable acts. He was once again, as had been the case two years before, held responsible for taking part in the plot to burn New York following the Battle of Brooklyn Heights.

We cannot know the thoughts that occupied his mind as he stood before this court martial. The officers assembled there were certainly no jury of his peers, and there would be at best a flimsy opportunity for him to defend the charges against him. He must have wondered what would become of his wife and baby, for there could be little doubt about the forthcoming verdict. There would be no parole and assignment to interpret for the Germans this time. He knew that he was guilty of several of the accusations, and that it took but one to convict him. Conviction was the end of the line; no appeals were permitted in military courts. The decision of the officers would be final. And they were obviously in no mood to be charitable or to wipe the slate clean.

The verdict was predetermined from the start, and Salomon was sentenced to be hanged by the neck until dead at sunrise the following day, August 11, 1778. He was returned to The Provost to await his fate in the morning.

As was revealed on many occasions, the slim Pole was an enterprising and clever man. He made it a practice to plan ahead

42

and was usually well equipped to meet whatever crisis might confront him. This was to prove to be no exception. He had known for some time before his actual arrest that imprisonment was near at hand, and he had armed himself, but not with a gun. He reasoned that if he were taken into custody, there was little that he could do to forestall conviction. So he conceived a plan that was designed to permit him to escape. Salomon concealed several gold coins in his clothing and, sometime during the night, bribed one or more of his guards and gained freedom. Another gamble had paid off.

Breaking out of The Provost was one thing. Leaving New York City without detection was clearly another. Redcoat troops numbering 10,000 were quartered there. Manhattan Island was an armed enemy camp. The American lines were to the North at Dobbs Ferry.

As he began his dash to freedom, Salomon found that a lack of moonlight was to his advantage. His greatest fear was that his uncontrollable coughing might give him away. But luck was on his side that night as he managed to avoid British sentries and guards on his way to the outskirts of the city.

Profoundly tempted as he was, Salomon dared not stop by his home to let Rachel know of his escape; he knew this would be the first place he would be sought when the guards found him missing from his Provost cell.

Barking dogs, his increasing fear of discovery and his will to live all spurred him on. At dawn, he had still managed to remain free. He looked for a safe place to hide and rest. Perhaps it was with a sympathetic Dutch farm family, or in a haystack, or in one of the caves that were then to be found in Manhattan's wooded hills. How, history tells us not, but Salomon was somehow able to evade the British patrols.

The next night, hungry and exhausted yet sensing that his plan might well succeed, he continued his flight to the North.

He eventually reached the Bronx shore of Spuyten Duyvil Creek, now dredged so that ocean going vessels can pass to the sea, but at the time little more than a shallow stream. Once across it, he left Manhattan Island, The Provost and his family behind.

It was about fifteen miles of rural landscape between the present location of the city of Yonkers, where Salomon found himself, and the Patriot lines at Dobbs Ferry. Here, raiding parties from both sides and occasional highwaymen were to be reckoned with. Westchester County of 200 years ago was not a great deal safer than Congress Hall had been for Salomon. His good luck never left him through a second night. Finally he made contact with an advance party of the Continental Army. Much to his surprise and delight, Salomon discovered that Alexander MacDougall, one of the "Sons of Liberty" whom he had joined in opposing the oppressive acts of the Crown years before, was the commanding general of this region. MacDougall had himself been exposed to William Cunningham's "hospitality" at The Provost in 1770.

Salomon was at last free, but the cost had been tremendous. He was penniless, without friends or family, and had no idea as to what he was going to do. His first thoughts were to take up arms and stay with MacDougall's troops as a foot soldier. Perhaps he could help out in some way with feeding the men, or in some other military capacity. But it did not take him long to determine that there was a greater need that he might meet, and that the front lines were not to be his battlefield.

The Continental Congress had returned from its exile in York and was once again in session in Philadelphia. Salomon learned from MacDougall and his own observations that American soldiers were poorly fed, equipped and clothed. Anyone could tell that it was a lack of money, not a lack of mettle, that was frustrating the Americans. Money was something that Haym Salomon understood. Here was an opportunity for him to make a contribution. Philadelphia was the place to go.

He was granted a pass to undertake the trip to the capital and set out on foot to travel the one hundred miles to his goal. In doing so, he retraced in reverse the British withdrawal to New York that had taken place only a few weeks previously. As the distance between him and his beloved Rachel and Ezekiel increased, he was undoubtedly lonely. But Haym Salomon knew that he was a man of destiny. He knew where he had to go.

8 *To Philadelphia*

The Philadelphia that Haym Salomon entered in late August of 1778 was an active and prosperous city. Departure of the British and subsequent re-occupation by the Americans had actually caused a minimum of confusion. Those who had sold provisions and produce to the Redcoats now offered their wares to the Patriots. Business went on as usual with the exception that there were fewer fancy dress balls, and a glaring absence of elegant crimson colored uniforms. The Pennsylvania State House that we now know as Independence Hall had been used as a military hospital during the time the English were in command. Before the Continental Congress could resume its deliberations, it had to be reconditioned. All around him, perceptive Haym Salomon observed the lingering traces of recent British rule. Horses had been quartered in schools, churches and meeting houses; homes of those suspected of sympathizing with the revolutionists had been looted and set on fire.

But of one thing there was no doubt: Philadelphia was where the action was, and Salomon found himself a displaced person in immediate need of employment and lodgings. He was a stranger and a foreigner seeking welcome in an unknown place.

His father-in-law, Moses Benjamin Franks, had business connections in the Quaker City, and it is probable that the newcomer from New York enjoyed certain resulting advantages. While Salomon's monetary assets had been left behind, and he could only guess whether or not they had been seized by his British captors, he still possessed his greatest treasure: his ability to conduct himself in commerce in an honest and profitable manner.

From the time of his youth in Poland, Salomon had been a devout adherent to the Jewish faith, so it is not unusual that he would have inquired as to the location of the local synagogue. He learned that the Congregation Mikveh Israel met in the home of Joseph Cauffman in Cherry Alley off Third Street. He went there.

Within the membership of his small temple, Salomon was to make many friends who were to remain his close associates during the balance of his life. The Gratz brothers, Bernard and Michael, were influential local merchants who helped this outsider become acquainted around Philadelphia. They introduced him to the men who frequented the coffee houses where much of the commercial activity of the city was carried out. A grain dealer named Jacob ben Casro was also able to lend a hand, to provide additional opportunities for the newly arrived broker to prove his ability to deal effectively in his chosen profession. Along with Isaac Moses, Benjamin Levy and Jonas Phillips, the families of the Congregation Mikveh Israel welcomed him into their homes and into Philadelphia's thriving business community.

Salomon quickly learned that the waterfront was the hub of that city's trade center. The Delaware River yielded access to the Atlantic Ocean and, in spite of risks of the British blockade, American ships of all sizes and descriptions crowded the docks and moorings. The hustle and bustle of the wharves was compounded by the fact that one could hear numerous languages blended among the traders' conversations and dealings. Ship's captains from ports all over the world dropped anchor here to discharge and sell their cargoes to the highest bidders. Then, after loading their holds with goods from the Colonies, they would set sail again and attempt to run the blockade.

The little Jewish broker must have appreciated the fact that he now might continue to serve here as an agent for supplies, as he had in New York City. He even may have found that his reputation as an effective and honest middleman between buyer and seller had preceded him to Philadelphia. It surely did not go unnoticed that he was related by marriage to the prominent Franks family, and it is probable that funds were advanced which soon enabled him to open offices on Front Street near the busy coffee houses.

These establishments dispensed more than coffee; they served as centers of trade where information was exchanged, and where brokers, traders, bankers and merchants met to conduct their business.

Again, Salomon's knowledge of foreign and domestic commerce must have served him well. His ability to converse in several languages gave him a decided edge when dealing with merchantship captains from faraway lands. No doubt he learned quickly that there were those who attempted to increase their own fortunes at the expense of the struggling war effort. And he found that there was little confidence, even among sincere patriots, in the paper money issued and endorsed by the Continental Congress.

These bills were so poorly regarded and valued that many shopkeepers refused to accept them in payment. There were smiths, tailors, farmers, saddlers, buttonmakers, chandlers and glovers who insisted upon "hard" money for their goods and services. The phrase, "not worth a Continental," accurately described the lack of trust many people had in the ability of the newly formed government to redeem its paper dollar bills.

Trade was carried out in a wide variety of foreign coin and money, and Haym Salomon was well equipped to deal in this medium of exchange as he soon demonstrated.

Salomon had three priorities at the time: to attempt to recover or replace his financial assets left behind in New York, to reunite his family, and to build a new business career in Philadelphia to the point that he could materially aid the Patriot's cause. He was to be successful in achieving two of these three goals.

In the Library of Congress today, located in the National Archives of the United States, the official records and original documents of the government are available to scholars and others interested in tracing the history of the nation to its primary sources. The *Journal of the Continental Congress II* may be examined there. Beginning on page 840 of papers identified as Number 41, Folio 58, there appears a petition signed by Haym Salomon. It is quaint in that it reflects the English language as written by educated persons in the formal manner of Colonial times. Some of the words may appear peculiar, and some of the spelling may seem strange, but the meaning comes through clearly. Here is a man who has been through terrible times, but whose pride and courage nevertheless have survived.

"To the Honorable the Continental Congress:
The memorial of Haym Salomon late of the City of New York, Merchant, Humbly Sheweth.

That your Memorialist was some time before the Entry of the British Troops at the said City of New York and soon taken up as a spy and by General Robertson committed to the Provost — That by the Interposition of Liet. General Heister (who wanted him on account of his knowledge in the French, Polish, Russian, Italian etc. Languages) he was given over to the Hessian Commander who appointed him in the Commissary Way as purveyor chiefly for the Officers—That being at New York he has been of great service to the French and American prisoners and has assisted them with Money and helped them to make their Escape — That this and his close connexions with such of the Hessian Officers as were inclined to resign, and with Monsieur Samuel Demezes, has rendered him at last so obnoxious to the British Head Quarters that he was already pursued by the Guards and on Tuesday the 11th inst, he made his happy Escape from thence—This Monsieur Demezes is now most barbarously treated at the Provost's and is seemingly in danger of his life. And the Memorialist begs leave to cause him to be remembered by Congress for an Exchange.

Your Memorialist has upon this Event most irrevocably lost all his Effects and Credits to the amount of five or six thousand Pounds sterling and left his distressed Wife and a Child of a Month Old at New York waiting that they may soon have an opportunity to come out from thence with empty hands.

In these Circumstances he most humbly prayeth to grant him any Employ in the way of his Business whereby he may be enabled to support himself and family. —And your Memorialist is in duty bound etc. etc.

Haym Salomon

Phila. Aug. 27, 1778.''

Records available to us today do not indicate that any action was ever taken by the Continental Congress on Salomon's poignant plea. It is probable that he expected no more from a governing body which was itself on the brink of bankruptcy. The nearly insolvent Congress had enough trouble paying its own bills without being burdened with the personal problems of a Jewish merchant who recently fled New York. The Board of War routinely received such petitions to Congress and, just as systematically, filed them.

While unable to gain any aid from the government, Salomon soon had some good news. An arrangement was made whereby his young family could depart from New York.

It was not long before Rachel was able to take their baby, Ezekiel, and make her way to join her husband in Philadelphia. What a happy reunion this must have been! Their home was gone, probably confiscated by the British to house Redcoat troops, a fortune estimated at $30,000 was lost to them forever, and the only possessions either had were what they were able to carry or wear on their backs. But, they had each other, and one can imagine Salomon going to the rented building which served as a synagogue and humbly thanking God for bringing his family safely together again.

Robert Morris Seeks Haym Salomon's Assistance.

9 Robert Morris

In reality, we were engaged not in just one war now, but two. The land struggle, involving troops under Washington's command, was designed to harrass and confuse the Redcoats through swift strikes and strategic withdrawals. With a population somewhat less than one-third that of Great Britain, and with a large number of Americans openly opposed to the war effort, the Patriot forces faced serious disadvantages. Foremost of these was an obvious lack of adequate economic resources, a condition which was to plague them well into the following years, even after the end of armed hostilities, as Salomon discovered.

The Americans of course, were not entirely lacking in advantages, and these were capitalized upon whenever possible. For example, they were in a position of defending their own homes on their own soil. This served to force the British to bring the war to the Colonies, to move massive materiel and men over sea routes often greater than three thousand miles. In spite of being outnumbered, the Continental Armies were usually able to hold their own on the several fronts of the land war.

The naval war was another matter.

Boasting the most formidable sea power in the world, Britain ruled the waves. America was obliged to rely upon a vastly smaller improvised navy which had a most difficult time challenging the royal fleet. Naval superiority was to provide the British with an advantage of tremendous value. Freedom to use the sealanes was vital to the Colonial cause, as the Patriots were dependent on shipping to carry out both domestic commerce and foreign trade. With their population extending along a thousand miles of eastern seaboard, the Americans soon felt the full impact of disruption caused by the English warships.

Salomon's office on Philadelphia's Front Street was close enough to the waterfront that he had the advantage of daily contact with the captains and traders who braved the running of the British sea blockade. The official United States Navy had been created on September 2, 1775, and the first four warships were commissioned the following month. Esek Hopkins was the ranking officer of this small fleet, but it soon became progressively apparent that a young lieutenant named John Paul Jones was the most daring and successful naval commander. His skill and bravery combined to result in the sinking or capturing of twenty-two ships of the Royal Navy during 1776 alone.

An estimated two thousand privately owned vessels joined the American Navy in attacking British ships during the course of the Revolutionary War. These privateers are credited with seizing or destroying over $18 million worth of warships, merchantmen and cargo. They had been authorized by the Continental Congress to prey upon the English wherever and whenever they could find them on the high seas. Any goods or ships they captured were theirs to keep as prizes of war.

Salomon divided his daylight hours between his Front Street office and the nearby coffee house. He served as a broker, buying and selling for a commission, both foreign and American currencies. He provided his talents as an agent for the trading of merchandise, but acted on his own as a dealer in various commodities and goods.

On occasions, he financially backed the captains and owners of privateers and blockade runners. Salomon shared in their spoils when their raids against the British were successful.

Salomon became increasingly concerned about his recurring cough. He had no choice but to seek medical help once again. A doctor confirmed that the original diagnosis of tuberculosis was correct. Salomon was then admonished—his health, his life were in grave jeopardy if he did not slow down the pace of his affairs and take life easier. It was typical of Salomon that the warning, in fact, spurred him on to do just the opposite.

The broker must have sensed that his days were numbered, and he decided to compress a lifetime of service into such time as he might have left.

He increased the size of his Front Street office and took on a partner, a Scotsman named MacRae. Salomon then rented the remaining portion of the structure to house his family, now grown to four with the birth of his first daughter, Sallie. Rachel must have been elated by the rapid growth of his business. But she certainly was equally distressed as she observed his health deteriorating under the prolonged intensity of his business efforts. It was not long before he was considered by most to be a rich man; it appeared as if he had a magic-like ability to breathe success into every venture he undertook. As his physical condition worsened, he continued to ignore his doctor's advice. Relentlessly, he drove himself even harder.

It seemed for a while that the struggle for independence might end in sudden victory, with General Burgoyne's surrender of his Redcoat troops at Monmouth, but actual events proved this to be only wishful dreaming.

Inflation reached the point that Continental currency was practically worthless. The British then cleverly compounded the problem by counterfeiting the Colonists' paper money and flooding the land with these fake bills in an attempt to further destroy the citizens' confidence in their new nation. It became a tremendous struggle just to keep the government from becoming bankrupt.

Salomon was aware of the support being given by the French. He heard how Benjamin Franklin had brought about a diplomatic triumph in convincing the French to send a steady supply of soldiers, munitions and bills of exchange across the Atlantic. He knew of the French Navy's successful efforts in thwarting the British blockade. He determined that they might need someone to act as their official representative in America. He believed that he was fully capable of serving in this capacity.

Dealing in bills of exchange was a highly specialized skill, dependent upon the broker's knowledge of the terms and conditions of the notes and his reputation for honesty and promptness in meeting business obligations. Salomon soon became recognized as one who would endorse such bills, and as one whose guarantee was such that he would later back his signature with hard cash, no matter which side won the war. Those who daily conducted their business in the coffee house turned to this dynamic man to be their agent in countless important financial transactions.

The French soon established headquarters in Philadelphia and set up garrisons in Rhode Island and New Jersey. Haym Salomon's fluency in the French language proved of value in working with these allies. His service shortly came to the attention of the French Minister, the Chevalier de la Luzerne. It was not long before Salomon was appointed official Paymaster General of the French Army and Navy in America and became Luzerne's financial advisor and counselor. His efforts were to further assist in funding General Lafayette's army with loans to purchase needed horses, saddles, food and arms until long-delayed supplies could arrive from France.

Records indicate that Salomon made personal loans to both the Spanish and French ambassadors to tide them over in meeting their expenses. He came to the rescue of Dutch officials who, in a similar manner, found themselves short of cash due to the effective British blockade.

When denied by Congress the funds he needed to continue the military effort necessary to successfully wage the war, General George Washington had meanwhile turned to Robert Morris. It was a desperate Washington who appointed Morris Minister of Finance "with the full power to raise the money needed to carry on the war."

Morris was responsible for paying the government's bills. He would accomplish this partly through the sale of tobacco, hides and agricultural products from the Colonies which had been provided in the place of hard cash. He also sold great amounts of British goods captured by privateers, and took a commission for the young government's treasury. He soon became aware of the talents and good name of Haym Salomon and suggested to mutual friends that the two should confer and discuss their common cause.

The exact details of Haym Salomon's initial meeting with Robert Morris are unknown to history, although such an association seems today to have been unavoidable. Morris and Salomon had much in common, in addition to their shared desire to aid their adopted land in gaining its freedom from Great Britain. America's first Minister of Finance was an Englishman who had left his birthplace in Liverpool at the age of 14 to sail to the Colonies. He served as a low-paid clerk in a Philadelphia commercial house and, even at such an early age, showed evidence of future promise in the field of finance. His father, a nailmaker, died when Morris was 21 and left his son $7000, a minor fortune at the time. The young Robert Morris soon was acclaimed as a force to be reckoned with in the business life of Colonial America. He was shortly one of the major shipowners and importers of the times, a man with interests and important connections all over the world. His wealth and extensive land holdings made him a logical choice as a delegate to the First Continental Congress.

Morris was neither an early nor an enthusiastic advocate for completely severing all ties with Great Britain. He knew that war would inevitably follow such a move and realized that the Colonists were as yet inadequately prepared for armed conflict with the military might of King George III. He argued that further negotiations would buy precious time—time needed to better plan the strategies of the Revolution to come. He debated the issue with vigor and served as a spokesman for those delegates against premature action. Then, when the resolution for independence was voted upon on July 2, 1776, his ballot was cast opposing the motion. After the votes were counted and the question resolved,

Morris, in good faith, endorsed the majority decision and placed his name alongside the other Patriots who cosigned the Declaration of Independence.

In doing so, he placed a price on his head. Robert Morris now became an instant candidate for British revenge.

10 *Private Stock*

The American Revolution and the uprising of the colonists became a symbol of optimism and inspiration for oppressed people in other lands. The cause of human rights and freedom, so eloquently expressed in the Declaration of Independence, was translated and read wherever men longed to be free. For the first time in recorded history, a great nation had formed a new government in which supreme power rested in voting citizens who then elected representatives to serve their needs. It was truly a remarkable experiment that the United States had embarked upon, a unique federal system of government designed to minister a land area so vast and unpopulated. Only a few years later, another exceptional document, a written Constitution, was ratified and became the basic law of the nation.

Haym Salomon and others were to provide the funds to bring about what has been called a "dislocation of authority" in an aristocratic and privileged social structure. It was not long before more liberal voting requirements were adopted and special advantages once only afforded large land owners were ended as their extensive estates were broken up. The prior criminal code became more humane, and prisons operated along the lines of The Provost became only a depressing memory of the past. An established national church, so common in the Europe of the time, gave way to religious freedom. In this new democracy, Jews, Protestants and Catholics could worship as they pleased, where they pleased, without fear of restraint or governmental interference.

Though by no means perfect, the newly created United States of America of two hundred years ago provided a unique climate for the growth of democracy and equal opportunity.

Morris told Salomon of his problems raising money for Washington's needs, and this provided the Polish Colonist with the opportunity he had been seeking. Now, he could make a clearcut contribution to the land of his choice. Now, he could bring to bear all the lessons he had learned over the years in dealing with financial matters. Now, he could fulfill his destiny.

His health seemed improved as he attacked the gigantic assignment given him by Morris. Perhaps the knowledge that he was making a major effort and that his energies were so deeply appreciated tended to provide a temporary relief from his sickness.

As Robert Morris received more and more demands for funds, he found himself continually turning to Salomon for aid. The Diary that Morris kept during this period, now preserved in America's National Archives, contains over seventy references to Salomon. And each entry in itself might well tell the tale of a successful military action, hungry and cold troops provided with food and warm clothing, bills paid and commitments met because of the untiring efforts of the little Jewish broker on Front Street.

The fact of the matter is that this was not solely a war waged by soldiers and naval forces. It was a combined action of civilians and the military, each dependent upon the other for support and encouragement. Without the private citizens who, like Haym Salomon, risked their fortunes as well as their necks, it is doubtful that victory would have been achieved. Salomon's assistance was not limited to those in uniform.

58

Diaries and letters of a number of major Revolutionary War figures are available to scholars for study today. References to Haym Salomon and his generosity may be found in many of these preserved documents. James Madison, for example, has been called the "Father of the Constitution" and served two terms as President of the United States. He wrote of Salomon as his "private benefactor." In a letter to Edmund Randolph, at one time Governor of Virginia, Madison described himself as a "pensioner" of Salomon's, and the *Writings of James Madison* contain the following passage which details the sentiments of this future President:

> "I am almost ashamed to reiterate my wants so incessantly to you, but they begin to be so urgent that it is impossible to suppress them. The kindness of our little friend in Front Street, near the coffee-house, is a fund which will preserve me from extremities, but I never resort to it without great mortification, as he obstinately rejects all recompense. The price of money is so usurious, that he thinks it ought to be extorted from none but those who aim at profitable speculations. To a necessitous Delegate he gratuitously spares a supply out of his private stock."

Madison was by no means alone in his obligations to his "little friend in Front Street." Thomas Jefferson, John Paul Jones, Benjamin Lincoln and General von Steuben were all aided from Salomon's "private stock" in the payment of their personal debts. He also loaned money to Governor Thomas Mifflin of Pennsylvania, to James Wilson, the first signer of the Declaration of Independence and America's earliest Federal Judge, to General Arthur Saint Clair, the original Governor of the Northwest Territory, to Edmund Randolph and to Robert Morris himself.

Other recipients of Salomon's financial assistance, all documented by contemporary records on file today in the Library of Congress, include such Patriot heroes as Arthur Lee, Joseph Jones, John F. Mercer, Joseph Reed, Major William McPherson and still another eventual President, James Monroe.

These cash advances were not only free of interest but were also made with the full knowledge that any potential payment would be made a long time in the future, if at all. Financial distress was a condition which affected the majority of those working night and day in the cause of freedom. Salomon totally believed in final victory for General George Washington and his fighting forces. He placed his entire fiscal resources at their disposal, and there is evidence that whole regiments of the Continental Army were supported by funds loaned from his accounts.

General Benedict Arnold, the brilliant American military leader who later disgraced himself by turning traitor and attempting to betray his own men at West Point, was also among those receiving support from the Polish Jew. It must have come as a major blow when Salomon later learned of the treachery of his former Philadelphia friend.

But this did not serve to shut off the flow of cash to needy Patriots, even though the broker's own assets were at times perilously reduced by his generosity. He acted out of a sincere desire to do all that he could to help those impoverished Americans who came to him with outstretched hands.

11 *A Triumvirate of Patriots*

Robert Morris became a frequent caller at Salomon's Front Street office. His visits were rarely social and the urgency with which he spoke told of the seriousness of his missions. Morris' diary in this period often refers to his meeting with Salomon as well as Washington to review financial matters. Notations such as the following were typical:

> "May 8, 1782
> I sent for Mr. Haym Salomon.
>
> June 25, 1782
> Mr. Haym Salomon came to inform me that he can buy Bills.
>
> July 1, 1782
> Haym Salomon the Broker informs me that he is applied to by Sundry Persons to sell Bills. I desired him to procure me Customers.

July 10, 1782
Haym Solomon came respecting Bills.

August 27, 1782
I sent for Salomon.

August 28, 1782
Salomon the Broker came and I urged him to leave no stone unturned to find out Money—or the means by which I can obtain it."

A story is still told in Philadelphia of a request for funds which was so pressing that it interrupted the observance of Yom Kippur, the Day of Atonement and holiest day of the year for those of the Jewish faith. The account relates that a knock on the door of the rented Congregation Mikveh Israel startled the worshippers as they were praying, asking for God's forgiveness and mercy. This was unheard of, to interfere in the religious life of others. But the knocking continued.

We are told that the door was opened, and a messenger asked for Haym Solomon. He had been sent by Robert Morris with the appeal that Solomon sell for him two Bills of Exchange amounting to $20,000. Yom Kippur is such a holy day that even the idea of money, let alone actual business transactions, is forbidden. The rabbi must have thought that Salomon had departed from his senses when he asked to speak to the people of the synagogue. As it became apparent that the broker wanted to discuss monetary matters, one can imagine the disbelief and anger among the congregation. But Salomon persisted, so the legend goes, and was so persuasive in his plea for the funds to purchase the Bills that he was able to subscribe the money in a few minutes. He is credited with buying a three thousand dollar share himself.

Formal records do not support that such an act took place on Yom Kippur; if it did, then still another Bicentennial anecdote can be added to those enriching American history through the deeds and sacrifices of our Colonial ancestors.

Salomon's family increased by another daughter this year as Deborah joined Ezekiel and Sallie, and the combined office and home on Front Street echoed with children's laughter and games.

It was in 1781, a year earlier, that the pivotal battle of the entire Revolutionary War was fought, and Haym Salomon is believed to have played a significant role in assuring its success.

New York City was the original target for the attack. General George Washington and the French Count de Rochambeau had planned to launch a joint strike against the British forces stationed there, in a bold attempt to recapture the city and turn the tide of the war. Sir Harry Clinton commanded His Majesty's northern armies as well as the New York garrison which for five long years had served as a major threat to victory in the War for Independence. The most massive English army in America was Clinton's, while Lord Charles Cornwallis was the general in charge of the southern Redcoat troops at Yorktown, in Virginia.

New York and Yorktown have similar names, but their comparison as military bases bears little likeness.

New York City was a well-fortified armed camp. It would have taken a major military force with superior manpower and weapons to force it to surrender. Yorktown, on the other hand, had been recently occupied by Cornwallis. It presented a much more inviting target.

With France now in the war and both French soldiers and ships available to Washington, a grand plan was developed. A powerful French fleet under the command of Count de Grasse was to sail for America. The aggressive French admiral would have the option of supporting Washington's attack on either New York or Yorktown. It was decided to have the Americans and French simulate an offensive against Manhattan, and then quickly march the five hundred miles South to engage Cornwallis in Virginia. De Grasse would meanwhile blockade the mouth of the York River and Chesapeake Bay and seal off any possible British escape routes by sea. The plan was so secret that neither Washington nor Rochambeau had initially told their own officers what was about to take place. There was the seemingly ever-present matter of finance, however. Washington would have to raise another $20,000 to pay the expenses of leading his army to Yorktown and a possible end of the war.

From his headquarters in Westchester County, North of New York City, Washington sent for Robert Morris. The two agreed that there was then only one man in America who was capable of providing such a sum in the short period of time required. It was necessary that Washington convince the French that he was now able to meet his financial obligations, even though this had not always been the case in the past. And, once again when the need was greatest, they sent for Haym Salomon. The rest is well documented history.

With Salomon's cash in hand, Washington joined Rochambeau and crossed the Hudson River on August 20. The British in New York City took their places against the anticipated attack. It was not until the main portion of the American and French armies had already crossed both the Hudson and Delaware Rivers that the English realized they had been fooled by Washington's strategy and cleverness.

The French fleet arrived on time. It was able to completely dominate the British Navy when, realizing that it would not be needed there for the attack that never came, it finally set sail from New York. Washington and Rochambeau arrived and established their siege positions on September 28, and the following three weeks saw fierce fighting along the outer lines of the tight circle drawn about the British.

At 2:00 p.m. on October 19, 1781, Great Britain suffered the greatest military defeat in its recent history. Two long lines of French and American troops, in their uniforms, both elegant and ragged, extended from the point of surrender. Cornwallis claimed that he was "sick" that day, and who can wonder; it must have been a strange sight to behold as the British and Hessian soldiers were ordered to stack their arms and become prisoners of war. General Charles O'Hara, Cornwallis' second ranking officer, surrendered his commander's sword to Washington's deputy, General Benjamin Lincoln.

Descriptions of the occasion relate that the British military band played a melody titled, "The World Turned Upside Down," while their troops were marching to surrender their arms. If this were the case, then the song was indeed an appropriate one in the manner it characterizes the situation. Cornwallis sent a brief note to Clinton in New York the next day with the following succinct message:

> "I have the mortification to inform your Excellency that I have been forced to give up the posts of York and Gloucester, and to surrender the troops under my command."

There was a loud and lengthy celebration in the streets of Philadelphia and every other major American community when the news of Washington's victory became known by the people who had struggled so hard for this good news.

One can imagine the smile of satisfaction that must have crossed Haym Salomon's lips when he reflected on the part that he had played in bringing about this tremendous accomplishment.

He soon discovered that victory did not decrease the demands on his services. In fact, feeding captured British troops and maintaining them as well as their guards became a new challenge. He learned that winning a peace can be as expensive and troublesome as winning a war.

Salomon also learned that Colonial men were not the only ones responsible for acts of bravery and encouragement performed by Americans in their struggle for freedom. Molly Pitcher's feats at Monmouth were still the talk of Philadelphia and, even then, Betsy Ross was being credited with providing General Washington with a unifying flag for his fighting forces. He may have heard tell of "Old Mom" Rinker who had quietly spied on General Howe's Redcoat regiments and later relayed her reports to the Americans cleverly concealed in balls of yarn.

Even before the initial skirmishes of the undeclared war had taken place, many Colonial ladies refused to purchase English linen or brew British tea. It was not uncommon, even in totally occupied cities, to have American women decline to entertain British soldiers or sympathizers in their homes.

Martha Washington, Abigail Adams and Dolly Madison are

names that bring to mind the roles played by many feminine colonists.

While it is true that only masculine names are to be found on the historic documents of the Revolution, an interesting comment appeared in the pages of the *Freeman's Journal* in 1776. It rather grandly stated the following:

> "The patriotic young women to prevent the evil that would follow the neglect of putting in the crops, joined the ploughs and prepared the fallows for the seed."

It must have been comforting to many a citizen soldier to realize that his farm or shop was in such strong and dedicated hands, however feminine, while he was at the front.

The Pennsylvania State House in Philadelphia was the site of the signing of the Declaration of Independence on July 4, 1776, but it was another 75 years before the wooden frame structure became known as Independence Hall. In 1781, an event took place here which may have attracted the attention of Haym Salomon. The Liberty Bell, first cracked in testing, was removed from its original location in the building and rehung in a clock steeple that had replaced the original tower. The inscription cast on the side of that bell is one no doubt familiar to Salomon, for it comes from the third book of the Old Testament, Leviticus. Taken from Chapter XXV, verse 10, it reads: "Proclaim liberty throughout the land, unto all the inhabitants thereof."

Documents available for study in the archives of the American Jewish Historical Society reveal that Salomon was by no means alone as a Patriot Jew in the Revolutionary War. The liberty called for in the Bible of the Hebrews was bitterly achieved. Unfortunately, most history books have neglected the role of Jews in the conflict. In fact, many Jews made massive contributions to the eventual victory.

Mordecai Sheftall of Georgia, as Commissary General of the Continental Army's southern forces, had full responsibility for obtaining food and ammunition for thousands of troops. He was later seriously wounded as he took a front-line position in

66

defending Savannah against a British attack. Another Jew who bore arms against the English with distinction was David Emanuel, elected to serve as Governor of Georgia in 1801, at the time Thomas Jefferson first took the oath of office as President of the United States. Emanuel had been yet another Jewish war Patriot.

There was Mordecai Noah of North Carolina, a wealthy man who turned over his personal fortune to General Washington and then served on the staff of Francis Marion, the "Swamp Fox" who harrassed the Redcoats in a number of skirmishes along the southern front of the war.

A young French Jew, Benjamin Nones, came to America from his home in Bordeaux to join the forces of Baron Johann de Kalb, a German General serving under Washington. Nones was commended for bravery and later promoted to major.

David Salisbury Franks, Dr. Philip Moses Russell, Reuben Etting, and Philip Minis are other Jewish Colonists who served with distinction. It has been estimated that as many as six hundred of the approximately three thousand Jews in America during the Revolutionary War took up arms for their chosen country.

Still, it is doubtful that history will assign to any the ranking role earned by Haym Salomon. He was the tree of strength upon which both Washington and Morris leaned in time of need. The three were to be described by President Franklin D. Roosevelt in 1941 as "this great triumvirate of patriots." On the eve of what was to be known as Pearl Harbor Day, he referred to Salomon and Morris in this manner:

> "Their genius in finance and fiscal affairs and unselfish devotion to the cause of liberty made their support of the utmost importance when the struggling colonies were fighting against such heavy odds."

Salomon Conducts Business in the Coffee House.

12 Victory and a New Nation's Needs

It is a grim fact of war that its cost lingers long after the smoke has cleared.

Victory at Yorktown and a general slowdown of the land war gave little relief to Salomon. More demands upon his ability to raise funds came daily, from a variety of sources. If he had hoped that he would now have more time to devote to his young family and his failing health, then he was to be severely disappointed. Congress kept turning to its Minister of Finance to pay its mounting bills, and Robert Morris inevitably sought out Haym Salomon for help. The military forces of several of the states were still on active duty. Others were being gradually disbanded. Some simply returned to their farms or civilian occupations without going through the formality of discharges.

Morris decided that he must devise a new way to assist the nation in meeting its financial needs. He received the approval of Congress to charter a National Bank of North America. With the

Federal Treasury practically bankrupt, he looked to France for capital. He soon learned that the French were unwilling to send a large loan, so, as when faced with other fiscal crises in the past, Morris sent for Haym Salomon.

The little broker on Front Street had almost reached the bottom of his own resources, but was able to scrape together $900 to deposit in the newly-formed Bank. In addition, he convinced friends and clients to deposit another $7000. When one realizes that Salomon's meager $900 made him the Bank's leading depositor, then the massive money problems facing the nation become even more glaringly apparent.

Salomon still carried on his daily business affairs at the coffee house. The British blockade had been lifted, and more ships from ports all over the world were dropping anchor in the Delaware River off Philadelphia's waterfront.

He became even more active in community affairs and was accepted into membership in the local Masonic Lodge. Since both Morris and Washington were also Masons, it is possible that he had discussed his plan to affiliate with the King Solomon Lodge Number Two with one or the other of them.

Salomon quite probably encountered in Philadelphia some of the same Hessian troops he had earlier convinced to desert their Redcoat regiments. If he did, he soon discovered that many had prospered in their new roles as farmers, after abandoning the risky profession of hired men-at-arms. They had found that Pennsylvania's rich Lehigh Valley was ideal for agriculture and had taken advantage of that State's offer of free acreage for former mercenary soldiers. The term "Pennsylvania Dutch" was in use even then to describe these and other German immigrants who had settled in this fertile region of the Colonies.

As a Jewish youth growing up in Poland, Salomon must have shared with these other newcomers a dream of land of his own on which to live and raise a family.

Under the Articles of Confederation, the Congress had no dependable sources of revenue. By the time that 1784 got under way, less than 15% of the $10 million that Congress had requested had actually been paid by the 13 States. Many wondered if the

Colonies would be able to remain united, so serious were the issues threatening them.

Morris said on one occasion that discussing money with the States was like preaching to the dead. It was that difficult to obtain funds.

At one point in 1783, Congress even went so far as to authorize its Minister of Finance to borrow against the loans from foreign governments before negotiations granting those loans had been completed. Only a timely and sizable advance from Dutch bankers saved the day. Few today appreciate just how close to complete fiscal collapse the nation was on many occasions. Denying Congress the power to tax the Colonies was a major factor in keeping the union from succeeding as originally planned.

Salomon was called upon to endorse and place his own good name and reputation behind French Bills of Exchange in April of this year, and published the following notice in the *Independent Gazette* printed in Philadelphia:

"HAYM SALOMON
Takes this method to acquaint all those who possess full Sets of Bills of Exchange drawn in his favor and endorsed by him on Monsieur Boutin, Treasurer of the Marine Department of France, that they shall, on application, have the money refunded; and for bills of the above description which may have already been sent to France, satisfactory assurance will be given to the proprietors that they shall be paid, agreeable to their relative tenors, in Paris, April 19."

By this public means, Salomon staked his own prestige and credit behind the French paper. Thus he triumphed over still another crisis in the financing of his adopted land.

During this year, the members of the Congregation Mikveh Israel realized that their rented synagogue was no longer adequate to meet their religious needs. Holy Day services were crowded, and increased membership underlined the fact that many Jews had left other cities during the long war to live in the nation's capital in Philadelphia. The quarters that were in use were insufficient, and something had to be done to improve this situation.

While many felt that building a new house of worship during such difficult times might be unwise, plans nevertheless went ahead to construct a new synagogue on a lot that had been purchased on Cherry Street.

Although construction costs were affected by the inflationary times, and money was being sought from him for a multitude of demanding needs, Salomon pledged to underwrite one-quarter of the total amount needed to build the new temple. He was later to serve as the Congregation Mikveh Israel's first member and to assist with presiding at services held there.

Gershom Mendes Seixas, America's earliest native-born rabbi, officiated at the dedication of the new synagogue. Salomon donated to the congregation a beautiful Sefer Torah, a scroll of the Five Books of Moses which he had imported from Europe.

During what were to be the last years of his life, Salomon's thoughts returned to his youth and to Poland. He had been unable to maintain contact with his parents while the Revolution was in progress, but in 1783 was successful in his efforts to reach them. While he was a man of letters and had himself often been used as an interpreter and correspondent, Salomon found it necessary to employ another to actually write to his parents. They could read only in Yiddish, and this was one language Salomon could not write!

A gold chain for his mother was enclosed in one of the first letters, and he was soon sending regular contributions of money. His father had never before had enough funds to pay the taxes then needed to be permitted to live safely in his Polish town. Through his son's gift, this was arranged and the proper rights were theirs. Relatives in Poland soon began to imagine ways that they might also benefit from their "rich American cousin."

Several relatives wrote to Salomon and asked to be provided yearly allowances and to be able to send their children to the Colonies where Salomon would educate them. He again employed someone to write still another letter in Yiddish to be sent to Poland to settle this new issue. First, to his parents, he expressed the "joy that I feel on receiving those letters so long wished for." He then went on to explain how difficult it would have been for him to succeed in America "not having any learning." He said that he would not have known what to do "had it not been for the languages that I learned in my travels, such as French, English, etc. Therefore, I would advise all my relations to have their children well-educated, particularly in general languages, and should any of my brothers' children have a good head to learn Hebrew, I would contribute towards his being instructed."

Then, to an uncle in England who asked that Salomon give him an annual allowance and educate his son in America, he wrote the following:

> "Your ideas of my riches are too extensive. Rich I am not, but the little I have I think it is my duty to share with my poor father and mother. They are the first that are to be provided for by me, and must and shall have the preference. Whatever little more I can squeeze out, I will give my relations, but I tell you plainly and truly that it is not in my power to give you or any relations yearly allowances. Don't you or any of them expect it. Don't fill your mind with vain and idle expectations and golden dreams that never will or can be accomplished. Besides my father and mother, my wife and children must be provided for. I have three young children, and as my wife is very young may have more, and if you and the rest of my relations will consider these things with reason, they will be sensible of this I now write. But notwithstanding this I mean to assist my relations as far as it lays in my power."

Salomon knew well of the demands on his private treasury, and certainly had no plans to misspend what little capital he had remaining there.

Benjamin Franklin, John Jay and John Adams were the American peace negotiators who finally sat down with the French and British to work out terms of the peace and end formally what

73

had become a world war. To a lesser or greater degree Spain, Holland, Austria and Russia had also been involved and signed the final documents on September 3, 1783. The terms of the Paris Treaty contained secret provisions which greatly favored the United States and are considered today to be a great triumph for the young nation. Franklin was later to observe, when asked about the document, "There never was a good war or a bad peace."

Salomon's health briefly seemed to improve, and he took steps to return to New York City and reestablish his brokerage business there. With the war over, he planned to enter into a partnership with Jacob Mordecai. In New York, they rented space in an office on Wall Street, not too far from the present location of the Stock Exchange. Their plans were to take advantage of New York's status as a free port and the increase in shipping that this would bring Manhattan's harbor.

It may have been that he took time while in New York to meet with old pre-war friends, to eat in one of the taverns he had known while a resident, or even to see a sight or two. It is doubtful that he would have been able to pass either the Old Sugar House or The Provost without a chill running up and down his back. So close had been his call!

13 *The Final Years*

Upon returning to Philadelphia, Salomon was informed of a situation which was causing much concern among the Jewish population. It was a problem involving their individual rights, privileges not yet guaranteed them in the Constitution or Bill of Rights. This dilemma pertained to the current Pennsylvania law which required that all members of the state legislature must, before being admitted to membership, "acknowledge the Scriptures of the Old and New Testament to be given by Divine Inspiration."

Since the New Testament is the Christian Bible and contains religous teachings which Jews cannot accept, they were by this law barred from ever serving in their state's government.

Salomon joined Philadelphia's Jewish community in signing a petition to the Pennsylvania Board of Censors that asked for removal of this provision of the law. They cited the many loyal Jews who had served in the cause of Pennsylvania's liberty and the loss of vital business to the city should Jews decide to live and do their business elsewhere. Their petition was successful, and the state's new Constitution is considered today to be a landmark in fairness and the respect for civil liberties that it provides.

The final days of 1784 saw Haym Salomon's health rapidly deteriorate. His earlier imprisonment in The Provost and the years of damage to his lungs by the gnawing of tuberculosis had finally taken their toll. He was not yet 45 years old. Rachel, at 22, had full responsibility for three young children, and another was due to be born in the Spring.

The Revolutionary War claimed one more victim on January 6, 1785, when Haym Salomon, a Patriot who neither carried a rifle nor wore a uniform, died.

An accounting of Salomon's estate at the time of his death showed that he had himself invested heavily in government securities. He left a large packet of Continental currency, treasury certificates and similar bills and notes. Their face value was estimated at the time at $353,729.33. When his partner, MacRae, set out to sell them for Mrs. Salomon's benefit, he discovered that their cash value had decreased considerably below the amounts printed on them. He could raise only $44,732 from their sale. Salomon's debts at his death were $54,292. He had given so much to help others that he had not been able to provide for his own wife and children.

His assets at one time may have made him one of the richest men in the Colonies; when he died, he left his family virtually penniless. Rachel was forced to return to New York to live with her family while she awaited the birth of her fourth child. When he was born, she named him Haym M. Salomon, in memory of her late husband. He never knew his father.

And his father never knew the Constitution, nor did he know of the Bill of Rights and the freedoms that were to be guaranteed all citizens. He never was to know that thirty-seven additional states were to join the original thirteen and swell the ranks to fifty. He never lived to see his adopted land become a giant world power, alternately respected and feared by other sovereign nations. He would never have the rewarding satisfaction of loving and being loved by his and Rachel's grandchildren.

Still, Haym Salomon left a legacy which many a more celebrated figure might well envy. He died knowing that he had personally provided the transfusions of money which were needed to keep the struggling United States alive during its infancy.

In Philadelphia, the *Pennsylvania Packet* printed this notice in its issue of January 11, 1785:

> "Thursday last, expired, after a lingering illness, Mr. Haym Salomons, an eminent broker of this city; he was a native of Poland, and of the Hebrew nation. He was remarkable for his skill and integrity in his profession, and for his generous and human deportment. His remains were on Friday last deposited in the burial ground of the synagogue, in this city."

It must be considered today as somewhat ironic that, even in his own time in his own community, the name of this financial genius of the Revolutionary War would be spelled incorrectly in the official newspaper notice of his death. This is not inconsistent with the manner in which his memory and affairs have been treated in the near two hundred years since his service to America was performed.

His young widow was now dependent on others to help her untangle Salomon's financial affairs. It becomes difficult today for anyone to understand why those whom he had aided so unselfishly during his lifetime failed to rally to Rachel's assistance in this time of her great need. But they didn't, and the wife of the "eminent broker" of Philadelphia's Front Street discovered that she was totally unprepared to face the task of coping with the details of her late husband's business dealings. The State Treasurer of Pennsylvania asked that she turn over to him additional certificates and securities held in Salomon's name. She complied with this request. She was informed later that they had been "lost," and she received no further accounting of them.

Those individuals to whom Salomon had generously loaned money or guaranteed notes were now either unable or unwilling to repay their debts and come to the aid of his surviving wife. It is indeed amazing and incredible to consider that Robert Morris did not immediately step in and personally reinforce Rachel's claims for compensation. He alone in government circles was capable of assembling the necessary support, but history does not record any such encouragement from the one most qualified to lend a hand.

Rachel reluctantly gave up her efforts to press demands for repayment of the money due Salomon's estate. Her lack of experience in the confusing world of high finance left her no other choice. She eventually married David Heilbron in New York City and, with his help and affection, resumed the task of raising her four children.

Haym M. Salomon followed his father's career and became a merchant. Ezekiel also entered the financial field and served as cashier of the United States Bank in New Orleans after a tour of active duty in the Navy. Sallie married Joseph Andrews in 1794, and Deborah married Simon Myers Cohen in 1801. Rachel was a grandmother prior to her thirty-fifth birthday.

Efforts to establish new claims in Salomon's name were again made in 1844 by his youngest son, Haym M. Salomon. Although he had never set eyes on his father, he was well aware of his namesake's contribution and was dedicated to proving the case for repayment of the nation's debt to the estate and heirs.

A strange series of events was to handicap his efforts.

The capture and burning of Washington, D.C., by the British in the War of 1812 destroyed a great deal of the remaining evidence of Salomon's loans. Papers documenting money advanced by Salomon mysteriously disappeared from the personal files of President John Tyler in 1845. In spite of sworn statements, records and letters from various knowledgeable sources, no affirmative action was ever taken by any of the Congresses which were to consider the requests for reimbursement. The family finally gave up in their attempts to collect from the government so generously sustained by their Patriot ancestor.

Tributes to Salomon's memory and contributions to the success of the Revolutionary War have been made in this century by Presidents Theodore Roosevelt, William Howard Taft, Woodrow

Wilson, Calvin Coolidge, Herbert Hoover, Franklin D. Roosevelt and John F. Kennedy.

Recent memorials in the Congress of the United States have reflected the increased interest generated by the nation's Bicentennial Celebration. Senator Hubert H. Humphrey of Minnesota, Senator Jacob Javits of New York and Congressmen George Danielson of California and Adlai E. Stevenson III of Illinois have all been leaders in the movement to provide recognition for Haym Salomon. These statesmen have served to focus attention on the unpaid debt of gratitude owed by all Americans to the memory of the man who served his adopted land so well.

Haym Salomon's Final Resting Place in Philadelphia.

14 Haym Salomon in Perspective

On March 25, 1975, 191 years after Haym Salomon's death, the United States Postal Service honored him as the third Revolutionary War hero of Polish birth to be saluted by the issuance of a commemorative stamp. Casimer Pulaski, Thaddeus Kosciuszko and now Haym Salomon thus were officially recognized by their adopted land for the contributions the three had made in the cause of American liberty.

The colorful Haym Salomon postage stamp was designed by California artist Neil Boyle. It bears the legend, "Financial Hero." This would mark only the second time in the 128 year history of the Postal Service that a printed message was to appear on the reverse side of a stamp under the glue. The inscription reads as follows:

"Businessman and broker Haym Salomon was responsible for raising most of the money needed to finance the American Revolution and later to save the new nation from collapse."

According to government sources, suggestions for a postage stamp to call attention to Salomon's efforts were first made in 1931 and renewed with regularity by various groups and individuals during the intervening 44 years. Emanuel Borden of the Haym Salomon Foundation is generally credited as the prime source of energy behind the issuance of the commemorative stamp and other memorials to the Polish hero.

Three other stamps were issued at the same time to honor other lesser known and rarely celebrated patriots of the War for American Independence. They pictured Salem Poor, a courageous Black militiaman who was cited for bravery at the Battle of Bunker Hill, Miss Sybil Ludington, a 16 year old who rode through the night rallying colonists to engage the British at Danbury, Connecticut, and Peter Francisco, a fighter of exceptional strength who joined the Continental Army at 15 and fought with distinction until the Redcoats surrendered at Yorktown.

In 1941, a statue was unveiled in Heald Square on Wacker Drive, in Chicago, Illinois, honoring three figures who wagered their fortunes and their lives in the struggle for freedom: General George Washington, Robert Morris and Haym Salomon.

The occasion for the dedication of the statue was the 150th anniversary of the approval of the Bill of Rights as the first ten amendments to the United States Constitution. It was, not so incidentally, the first statue of Washington that does not depict him alone. It is the work of the distinguished artist Lorado Taft.

The monument was completed as a result of the efforts of the Patriotic Foundation of Chicago and the distinguished Illinois attorney, Barnet Hodes. Of Polish and Jewish heritage himself, Hodes has long been active in civic, legal and Masonic affairs. He urged that the statue emphasize the fact that the Revolutionary War was fought and won by a combination of military genius and citizen soldiers from a wide range of ethnic and religious backgrounds.

Still another statue can be observed today in Los Angeles, California, where Salomon's likeness overlooks that city's MacArthur Park.

The sculptor who designed this larger-than-life monument was named Robert Paine and claimed the honor of being a direct descendant of the Patriot Thomas Paine of "Common Sense" renown. He died before the figure could be completed, and David Resnick put the finishing hand to the memorial. Resnick, at 92 years of age, still finds the time to frequently visit the statue and bestow a warm salute to the banker from Poland whose principal interest was an interest in his adopted country's future and well-being.

Perhaps the greatest monument dedicated to this distinguished man is not to be found in bronze or as a portrait on a postage stamp. It exists in the two hundred year history of continuous freedom in his chosen land. The youthful dreams of liberty and justice for all that Haym Salomon had in faraway Poland were encouraged by the faith of his fathers, and ultimately fulfilled many thousands of miles from his birthplace.

The roots from which this cutting had been taken were indeed strong. The grafting had produced a remarkable man, one whose contributions, devotion, example and quiet strength were to have an everlasting influence on millions of Americans in the years to follow.

Still, his name is unfamiliar to most today. His life was marked by personal sacrifices in his quest for freedom. He lived but 45 years, was only 32 when he arrived in New York City, and was less than 40 when he provided and organized the massive financial support that was to rescue and sustain this fledgling nation.

Haym Salomon died penniless and virtually unrecognized; his monumental efforts had been at the risk of his failing health and family's security.

On December 4, 1783, General George Washington reassembled his officers and addressed them at Fraunces' Tavern, which still stands at the corner of Pearl and Broad Streets in lower Manhattan. It is close to the location of Salomon's original New York brokerage house. No American, then or now, could positively state the specific memories running through Washington's mind as he met with his men for the final time as their commanding general.

But it is more than merely possible that the name of Haym Salomon held a place of major distinction in the great honor roll of which the Father of our Country spoke on that occasion. In farewell, Washington said: "With a heart full of gratitude, I now take leave of you, most devoutly wishing that your later days may be as prosperous and happy as your former ones have been glorious and honorable."

It had been a little more than two years earlier that victory over Cornwallis at Yorktown and ultimate freedom for the Colonies was achieved following a terse order to "Send for Haym Salomon!"

Additional Reading

Readers wishing to refer to additional texts describing Haym Salomon's life or Colonial times, may wish to direct their attention to the materials listed on this page. The author found many of them valuable, to a greater or lesser extent, in his research in the writing of "Send for Haym Salomon!" The basic facts of Salomon's life are known to historians, and some other authors have built biographical fictional accounts from these recorded events. The incidents related in this volume are, to the author's best available knowledge, accurate. He accepts full responsibility for any oversights or shortcomings which may have occurred.

American Heritage, the Magazine of History
   Various Issues; esp. Oct. 1966, Vol. XVII, No. 6
American Promise
   Sulamith Ish Kishov; Behrman House, 1947
American Revolution Bicentennial
   Mike Roberts Color Productions, 1975
The First American Revolution
   Clinton Rossiter; Harcourt Brace & World, 1956
General Washington's Son of Israel
   Charles Hart; J. B. Lippincott, 1937
The Great Rehearsal
   Carl Van Doren; Viking Press, 1948
This Great Triumvirate of Patriots
   Harry Barnard; Follett Publishing Co., 1971
Haym Salomon
   Shirley Garson Milgrin; Follett Publishing Co., 1966
Haym Salomon and the Revolution
   Charles Edward Russell; Cosmopolitan Book Corp., 1930
Haym Salomon, Patriot Without a Sword
   J. J. Myers; "World Over" magazine, issues of Feb.-May, 1973
Haym Salomon, Son of Liberty
   Howard Fast; Julian Messner Inc., 1941
Heroes of American Jewish History
   Deborah Karp; KTAV Publishing House, Inc., 1972
The Jews in America: A History
   Rufus Learsi; World Publishing Co., 1954
Jews in American Wars
   J. George Fredman and Louis A. Falk; Jewish War Veterans of the United States of America, 1954

Jews, Justice and Judaism
　　Robert St. John; Doubleday & Company, Inc., 1969
The Making of a Nation, LIFE History of the United States
　　Vol. 2: 1775 - 1789; Richard Morris and the editors of LIFE TIME
　　Inc., 1963
The National Observer
　　Various Issues; esp. Sept. 27, 1975, "A Nation of Nations"
Patriotism of the American Jew
　　Samuel Walker McCall; The Plymouth Press, 1924
Pilgrim in a New Land
　　Lee Friedman; Jewish Publication Society of America, 1948
Pilgrim People
　　Anita Libman Lebeson; Harper and Brothers, 1950
Seedtime of the Republic, the Origin of the Am. Tradition of Pol. Liberty
　　Clinton Rossiter; Harcourt Brace & World, 1953
This Liberty
　　Leon S. Rosenthal, Dorrance & Company, 1951.
TIME Magazine
　　Issue of "July 4, 1776" *Independence*; TIME, Inc., 1975
Unrecognized Patriots, the Jews in the American Revolution
　　Samuel Rezneck; Greenwood Press, 1975
The Writings of James Madison
　　Edited by Gaillard Hunt, 1900

Appendix

On this and the following pages will be found reproductions of documents and other historical material relating to the life and services of Haym Salomon. They have been gathered in this volume so as to provide readers with a more complete understanding of the impact of his contributions on American life.

Pictured above are the portraits of three American Patriots of Polish birth who have been honored on United States Postage stamps as heroes of the Revolutionary War. The Salomon stamp was issued in 1975 as one of a series depicting "Contributors to the Cause."

To the Honourable the Continental Congress

The Memorial of Hyam Solomon late of
the City of New York, Merchant

humbly sheweth — That Your Memorialist was some time
before the Entry of the British Troops at the said City of New
York, and soon after taken up as a spy and by General
Robertson committed to the Provost — That by the
Interposition of Lieut General Heister (who wanted him on
account of his Knowledge in the French, polish, Russian
Italian &c. Languages) he was given over to the Hessian
Commander who appointed him in the Commissary Way
as Purveyor chiefly for the Officers — That being at New
York he has been of great Service to the French & American
prisoners and has assisted them with Money and helped
them off to make their Escape — That this and his
close Connexion with such of the Hessian Officers as were
inclined to resign and with Monsieur Samuel Demeres
has rendered him at last so obnoxious to the British Head
Quarters that he was already pursued by the Guards and
on Tuesday the 11th inst. he made his happy Escape
from thence — This Monsieur Demeres is now
barbarously treated at the Provost's and is seeming by in
danger of his Life And the Memorialist begs leave to
cause him to be remembered to Congress for an Exchange
Your Memorialist has upon this Event most sincere
ly lost all his Effects and Credits to the amount
of Time or six thousand Pounds sterling and left his

distressed Wife and a Child of a Month old at New York
waiting that they may soon have an Opportunity to
come out from thence with empty hands —
In these Circumstances he most humbly
prayeth to grant him any Employ in the Way
of his Business whereby he may be enabled to
support himself and family — And Your
Memorialist as in duty bound &c.t

Philad.a Aug.t 25th 1778
Haym Salomon

This is the original Memorial sent by Haym Salomon to the Continental Congress in 1778 following his escape from New York
and flight to Philadelphia. It is to be found in the National
Archives of the United States in the Library of Congress.

HAYM SALOMON,
Broker to the Office of Finance,

HAVING procured a licenfe for exercifing the employment of Auctioneer, has now opened, for the reception of every fpecies of merchandife, his houfe, No. 22, Wall-ftreet, lately occupied by Mr. Anthony L. Bleecker, (one of the beft ftands in this city) and every branch of bufinefs, which in the fmalleft degree appertains to the profeffions of FACTOR AUCTIONIER and BROKER, will be tranfacted in it with that fidelity, difpatch and punctuality, which has hitherto characterifed his dealings

The houfe, in point of convenience and fituation, is exceedingly well calculated for the different kinds of bufinefs above mentioned: and he thinks it almoft unneceffary to affure thofe who may favour it with their orders, that the ftrickeft attention will be paid to them, and the utmoft care and folicitude employed, to promote their intereft.

The nature of his bufinefs enables him to make remittances, to any part of the world with peculiar facility, and this he hopes will operate confiderably in his favour, with thofe who live at a diftance.

A defire of being more extenfively ufeful and of giving univerfal fatisfaction to the public, are are among his prinnipal motives for opening this houfe, and fhall be the great leading principle of all its tranfactions.

By being Broker to the Office of Finance, and honored with its confidence, all thofe fums have paffed through his hands which the generofity of the French Monarch, and the affection of the Merchants of the United Provinces, prompted them to furnifh us with to enable us to fupport the expence of the war, and which have fo much contributed to its fuccefs and happy termination. This is a circumftance which has eftablifhed his credit and reputation, and procured him the confidence of the public, a confidence which fhall be his ftudy and ambition to merit and increafe, by facredly performing all his engagements.

The bufinefs will be conducted upon the moft liberal and extenfive plan, under the firm of HAYM SALOMON, and JACOB MORDECAI.

N. B. Part Cafh will be advanced, if required.

This is a reproduction of one of several advertisements which appeared in New York City newspapers following the end of the Revolutionary War. Salomon's health failed and he died prior to being able to actually open this Wall Street Office.

HAYM SALOMON
1740 — 1785
AMERICAN PATRIOT

THE HUMAN SPIRIT
HAS FLOWERED ON-
LY IN FREEDOM THE DY-
NAMIC REALITY OF OUR
WORLDCULTURE FLOWED
FROM ITS FIRST
DEMOCRACY

LET ALL AMERICANS AC-
CLAIM HAYM SALOMON
A PATRIOT A BENEFACTOR
OF HIS COUNTRY AN INCIT-
ER TO PATRIOTISM To MEM-
BERS OF HIS RACE TO HIS
COUNTRYMEN AND To LAT-
ER GENERATIONS·
IT LOOKS AS THOUGH HIS
CREDIT WAS BETTER THAN
THAT ? THE WHOLE THIRTEEN
UNITED STATES ? AMERICA·
ALBERT ·BUSHNELL· HART
PROFESSOR EMERITUS OF HISTORY OF HARVARD UNIVERSITY

Pictured here are two views of the Haym Salomon statue that is to be found in Los Angeles, California, in MacArthur Park. The work of Robert Paine, it bears witness to Salomon's role in America's beginnings.

ROBERT MORRIS · GEORGE WASHINGTON · HAYM SALOMON

★ ★ ★

THE GOVERNMENT OF THE UNITED STATES
WHICH GIVES TO BIGOTRY NO SANCTION TO PERSECUTION
NO ASSISTANCE REQUIRES ONLY THAT THEY WHO LIVE UNDER
ITS PROTECTION SHOULD DEMEAN THEMSELVES AS GOOD CITIZENS
IN GIVING IT ON ALL OCCASIONS THEIR EFFECTUAL SUPPORT
PRESIDENT GEORGE WASHINGTON 1790

★ ★ ★ ★

In Heald Square on Wacker Drive in Chicago, Illinois, stands a larger-than-life statue portraying General George Washington, Robert Morris and Haym Salomon. The grouping is intended to honor the role that civilians played in supporting the successful military effort.

91

Congressional Record

United States of America

PROCEEDINGS AND DEBATES OF THE 94th CONGRESS, FIRST SESSION

Vol. 121   WASHINGTON, TUESDAY, MARCH 25, 1975   *No. 50*

HAYM SALOMON REVOLUTIONARY PATRIOT

The SPEAKER pro tempore. Under a previous order of the House, the gentleman from California (Mr. DANIELSON) is recognized for 10 minutes.

Mr. DANIELSON. Mr. Speaker, today is the first day of issue by the U.S. Postal Service of a commemorative stamp to honor Haym Salomon, a great patriot of the American Revolution. Enscribed "Haym Salomon—Financial Hero," the stamp is one of four issued as a series to honor "Contributions to the Cause" and to commemorate the initial role they played in our American Revolution.

The stamp further commemorates the Bicentennial program for Haym Salomon, which was conducted by the Los Angeles District Council of the Jewish War Veterans of the United States on Sunday, January 26, 1975. The fine work of that Council, its auxiliary, and its friends has resulted in this recognition of Haym Salomon's magnificent work in furtherance of the American Revolution.

Haym Salomon, merchant, banker, and Revolutionary War financier, was born in Poland of Jewish-Portuguese parents in 1740. An advocate of Polish independence, he fled to England in 1771 and then to America, where he opened a brokerage office in New York.

He was in New York only a few months before he joined the Sons of Liberty, a group of revolutionary patriots, and was twice arrested and imprisoned by the British. Later, in Philadelphia, Salomon became financial agent in America for the French Government and was one of the leading dealers in bills of exchange and other securities. As a large depositor in Robert Morris' Bank of North America, Salomon contributed to maintaining the new government's credit. When Morris was appointed Superintendent of Finance, he turned to Salomon for help in raising the money needed to carry on the war and later to have the emerging nation from financial collapse. Salomon advanced direct loans to the government and also gave generously of his own resources to pay the salaries of government officials and army officers. With frequent entries of "I sent for Haym Salomon," Morris' diary for the years 1781–84 records some 75 transactions between the two men.

After the war, Salomon was almost penniless and died in 1785 before he could rebuild his business. Salomon, Morris and George Washington are the subjects of Lorado Taft's "Great Triumvirate of Patriots" monument in Chicago.

As we approach our Nation's Bicentennial, it is most appropriate that we pause to pay our respect to those who made freedom in America possible. We are greatly indebted to the band of American revolutionaries who broke the bonds of oppression and tyranny and secured the fortune of freedom to our people. It was an act of total dedication when the Signers of the Declaration of Independence, on July 4, 1776, adopted Thomas Jefferson's immortal words:

And for the support of this Declaration, with a firm Reliance on the Protection of divine Providence, we mutually pledge to each other our Lives, our Fortunes, and our sacred Honor.

This mutual pledge of dedication marked the dawn of free government for people in America and throughout the world. The thousands of patriots who joined the Signers also pledged their lives, their fortunes and their sacred honor. The great patriot whom we honor today, Haym Salomon, is one of these, for as he too accepted this pledge, he also carried the lead to insure the funds essential to the success of our American Revolution. He, too, pledged his life, his fortune, and his sacred honor.

This is but one of the many references in the Congressional Record of the United States to the contributions of Haym Salomon. Congressman Danielson of California here echoes the words of many Senators and Representatives over the years who have joined to praise his devotion and dedication.

Ford Times *magazine spotlighted the accomplishments of Haym Salomon in their issue of August, 1975. The illustration on this page by artist Pete Harrotos shows a young Salomon shortly after he arrived in Philadelphia. It is titled, "Financial Wizard of the Revolution."*

THE WHITE HOUSE

WASHINGTON

November 13, 1941

My dear Mr. Hodes:

The strength of the American cause in the War of the Revolution lay in the fact that in every critical phase of the contest the right leaders were raised up to perform whatever task needed to be done.

The incomparable leadership of Washington would have been nullified without the able support he received from key men in the various stages of the struggle out of which we emerged as a Nation.

Two financiers on whom Washington leaned heavily in the darkest hours of the Revolution were Haym Salomon and Robert Morris. Their genius in finance and fiscal affairs and unselfish devotion to the cause of liberty made their support of the utmost importance when the struggling colonies were fighting against such heavy odds.

It is, therefore, especially appropriate that this great triumvirate of patriots -- George Washington, Robert Morris and Haym Salomon -- should be commemorated together in Chicago. The memorial which you are about to dedicate will stand as an inspiration to generations yet unborn to place love of country above every selfish end.

Very sincerely yours,

Franklin D. Roosevelt

Honorable Barnet Hodes,
Co-Chairman,
Patriotic Foundation of Chicago,
Chicago, Illinois.

President Franklin D. Roosevelt is the author of the letter reproduced on this page. It expresses his feelings regarding the dedication of the statue of Washington, Morris and Salomon in Chicago in 1941, just a few days prior to the Japanese attack on Pearl Harbor and the beginning of World War II.

The Ketubah, *Marriage Contract of Haym
Salomon and Rachel Franks, New York, 1773.*

95

Waym Salomon
(Philadelphia)   Lancaster Feby 4th 1782

Dear Sir.

There is a number of Officers here
Belonging to Cornwallis's army, which are in great want of money
and must draw on New-York, but find it difficult to Sell their Bills
I have been apply'd too by Some of them to negotiate their Bills
for them. but the Scarcity of Cash has made me decline it, and
I now apply to you to Know if You will undertake to Sell their
Bills or if You will be concerned in the purchaseing of
them, and if I Should Send Bills to You if You will advance
money for them & Upon what terms, they at present Sell for
20 PCt discount. Major Gordon who commands here indorses their
Bills I think something very considerable might be made
by them could You fix upon Some methods how to get the
Money out of New-York and this I think You can easily do
from the connections which I am Informed You have at
Philadelphia. be so good as to return me an answer by the
post. as I Shall not come to any determination with them
untill I hear from You.

please to present my   Your most Obet Humle Sert
best respects at home   Joshua Isaacs

Joshua Isaacs   Philadelphia 7th Feby 1782.
Lancaster   Sir

                    Received Yours of the 4th Inst and
am very much Obliged to You, for Your information of
the Bills You mentioned, I agree with You in Opinion
that Something Considerable may be made by them

                    This It depends intirely in the manner
they are drawn. If they are drawn by the pay Master
Genl in favour of any particular Officers and Indored by their

From Haym Salomon's letter book, containing a
page of correspondence, 1782.